THESE SHARED HIS CROSS

✠

These Shared His Cross

STUDIES IN THE LAST DAY
OF THE LIFE OF JESUS

by

EDWIN McNEILL POTEAT

HARPER & BROTHERS PUBLISHERS

THESE SHARED HIS CROSS

FIRST EDITION

L-P

april 1953

Affectionately Inscribed
to my Son

CONTENTS

"I would know him in . . . the fellowship of his sufferings, with my nature transformed to die as he died."

Philippians 3:10 (Moffatt's Translation)

ACKNOWLEDGMENTS

The author wishes to express his appreciation to the following authors and publishers for permission to quote from their copyrighted works:

D. Appleton-Century Company. *Why Men Fight,* by Bertrand Russell.
Dodd, Mead & Company. *The Everlasting Man* and *Heretics,* by Gilbert K. Chesterton.
Henry Holt and Company, Inc. *Collected Poems,* by Mark Van Doren.
Alfred A. Knopf, Inc. *Malice of Men,* by Warwick Deeping.
The Macmillan Company. *Poems,* by W. E. Henley and *Liberality and Civilization,* by Profesor Gilbert Murray.
The Saturday Review of Literature. Poem by Ralph Friedrich.

Introduction

A year ago I wrote a book of devotional reflections on the experiences of those intimate associates of our Lord who followed him through the six days preceding his death.[1] The sequence outlined by Moffatt's *Everyman's Life of Jesus* provided the historical continuity of those studies, and an effort to recreate somewhat the states of mind that accounted for the behavior of his friends, provided the aim. The extraordinary tension created by uncertainty, fear, and distrust, resulted in the panic, the protest, and the betrayal; and finally caused the abandonment by most of them of their leader in his hour of death. At the same time, the conditions that produced panic in them, seemed to produce poise in him. As they felt the tension tighten, he, by an access of spiritual reinforcement that will always be both inexplicable and reassuring, was conscious of an easing of the strain, so that while "they all forsook him, and fled" the imminent terror, he accepted destiny with a steadfast spirit and at the last commended his soul confidently to his Father.

It so happened that the book was written during the "war of nerves." Shortly after the completion of the manuscript the blitzkrieg in Poland succeeded the psychological phase of the conflict; and, in spite of the horror of that opening act of aggression, a sigh of relief betokened the release of the tension that had so long constricted the nerves of the world. It was as if the world had agreed that since the thing had to happen sometime, it was better to have it happen soon, and thus sooner ended. The continuance of threat and uncertainty was driving men insane; the prospect of dying in a contest of arms was more alluring than living in a madhouse. The stoic calm

[1] *These Shared His Passion,* Harper & Brothers.

xi

of some of the belligerents now under the actual hammering of war is a testimony to the sense of relief that generally follows a nightmare of uncertainty.

This is one of the strange psychological responses to life that our deafening days present to us, and yet it is as old as life itself. The record of the closing day of our Lord's life reveals in miniature the same sort of mind. For six days the grueling anxiety concerning what was likely to take place tortured the hearts of his friends. And then the blow struck; he was caught between the casuistry of the religious hierarchs and the chicanery of the Roman hirelings, and condemned to death. It was a ghastly prospect that faced the fellowship that Friday morning, but there is evidence that it was easier to endure than the tautness of their uncertainty had been. Their reactions were varied. Some who had faltered in their loyalty fled. One whose disturbed mind had led him to the act of betrayal, sought escape from himself in suicide. Three women and one disciple—according to the account of John—saw the tragedy to its bloody end. Was there a sense of relief in the spirit of Mary when the sword that was promised her years before by Simeon (Luke 2:35) finally plunged into her heart?

But for the most part, the sense of release spent itself in flight. Once their minds were set free of uncertainty by the judgment of Pilate, wings were lent to the feet of Jesus' friends. Where some of them went will never be known. As a consequence of this all but unanimous retreat, we find that those who shared his cross, were not those who shared his passion. A new lot of characters find their way into the story, and most of them are without a name. And yet they appear in relation to his death in a way similar to that in which the others were related to his passion. The former group shared his passion but not the poise it brought him; the latter group shared his cross but not the redemption he brought the world.

It is this important fact that has induced a continuance of the type of study begun in the former book. We cannot enter into the experience of the Lord of Life without sharing his passion, but this means sharing it in a manner missed by those of an earlier day. "To the Christian who has apprehended the meaning of the Cross, these days may be the overture of a new Redemption, which shall ultimately be made possible only by those, who down the ages and to the end of time, have shared and will share the passion of the Son of Man."[2] Those concluding words demanded, in a sense, further pursuit of the idea of sharing the experiences of Jesus beyond the point of his passion, up to and through the experience of his death. But this involved, among others, two obvious difficulties. The former studies were an effort to come to a fresh understanding of the states of mind that induced certain acts. Fear very largely proved to be the cause of irrational and panicky behavior. It had a definite place in the betrayal of Judas, the denials of Peter, and even in the judgment of the Procurator. Mental fatigue in the house at Bethany, the restlessness of the deeply philosophical Thomas, the sense of frustration in the empirically-minded Philip, these were all elements in the individual and group reactions of his friends. But since those who shared the experience of his dying, as witnesses of the process that began in the praetorium and ended in the tomb of Joseph, are not known by name, and have left nothing but brief appearances on the scene by which they can be identified, it has been necessary to create for them in some cases a name, and in some a character. Legend has been busy with Simon of Cyrene, Joseph of Arimathea, Nicodemus, and the Centurion. For these four figures it is not difficult to gather, out of the known facts, either about them or the circumstances in which their lives were cast, a framework for each into which a character can be plausibly set. In the case of the man who scourged him, the women who lamented him, the two malefactors and the crowds that passed by, legend has been consistently silent. For them,

[2] *These Shared His Passion:* p. 131.

therefore it has been necessary to provide a "local habitation and a name." And due to the paucity of reference in the record, one has to rely entirely on the imagination. There is justification for this if violence is not done to the general direction in which the historic record moves and if the characters as delineated do not, of themselves, create the problems around which the discussion centers.

The second difficulty is more considerable. The Cross is the *punctum saliens* of the Christian gospel, and for this reason it has been reflected upon from every conceivable point of view. When an idea becomes established in thought, it almost inevitably runs through a well-defined cycle. As an experience it takes shape in an idea, as an idea it expands into a principle, as a principle it hardens into a dogma, as a dogma it takes refuge in an institution that has a vested interest in its advocacy or maintenance. It may issue finally in a symbolic form, and become the object of superstitious adoration itself. So what began as an idea that aroused to action becomes, at the last, an anesthetic that lulls to sleep.

The Cross has run this cycle, and to recover vitality to it, as an experience, is extremely difficult. If, however, it is a cosmic principle, it must be kept vital in human experience, kept as contemporary as the cosmos, indeed. And obviously this is not easy. The Cross, being an historic fact, has for most of us little more than historic interest and value. The Cross, as a principle hardened into dogma for us, loses its quality as a discipline for us, and when that happens its institutionalization and even its superstitious veneration are not far removed. See how the Cross has become a crucifix!

How can an experience of the Cross be induced? By the telling of a series of imaginary episodes, this book seeks to get back behind the theologizing of the Cross to the experience of it in the lives of several witnesses. To them it was not what it is to us, a part of the drama of redemption. On the contrary it was tragedy, stark and unrelieved. And yet it is not implausible to believe that in the cases here presented, the experience of seeing Jesus die, was to them the prelude to their ultimate redemption. Sharing the Cross is vastly more than seeing him die, as will be subsequently brought out. But the first step—the step that was taken before theologians and philosophers began talking about the Cross—was a sharing of his death as spectators. That must always, we think, be preliminary to sharing his Cross as redeemers, though such is the elemental purpose, on the human level, of the divine imperative as it presses on every Christian. "Whosoever doth not bear his own cross and come after me, cannot be my disciple." (Luke 14:27)

The Cross as a cosmic principle must encompass and redeem every aspect of experience. If it is a principle germane to the nature of reality, then it cannot be allocated in thought and experience to a few convenient segments of life. It supplies the meaning to *all* of life or to *none* of it. It gives meaning to goodness as well as to evil. It is related to sin only because life is sinful; it gives significance to godliness only because life can be godlike. For this reason these studies, which take up the characters in the order of their appearance in the record, deal with problems the characters present. The Cross therefore is set over against the cruelty of the scourger, the property of Simon, the family of the lamenting women, the life philosophies of the malefactors, the liberalism of one who passed by in the mob, the orthodoxy of two who buried him, and the military system under whose legal code he was crucified. Here the Cross is dealing with the processes of thought as well as the practices of conduct. Neither can be properly omitted if we are to understand it in its cosmic perspective and dynamic power.

We cannot, of course, escape the tragic aspects of the death of Jesus even though the tendency is to rationalize them till tragedy becomes glory. It is necessary in these pages, in order that the experience of our Lord be made vivid, to paint the scenes before us in vivid colors. They may even seem brutal.

But if this is the case, it is only with the intention that with the picture of his great anguish before us we may be able to probe the depths of our hearts to see if our own tragic hour will find us ready and willing to share his Cross, and in so doing to have some small part in redeeming the world from its unspeakable folly and sin.

CHAPTER ONE

Part One

THE PRAETORIANS

The Raven, so named by his fellow legionaries because his voice was singularly rasping, stirred lazily in the straw. The men of his company lay about him disposed in various attitudes and degrees of sleep. The sun was only just high enough to have begun pouring its lazy warmth into the open court, and as the light began its slow trespass across the sprawling figures, they began to stretch, sit up, yawn, and rub their heavy eyes. They had scarcely moved since the second watch when the noisy exit of two squads of the guard for emergency duty had disturbed their torpid slumber for a moment. They had known little comfort and less leisure since their arrival from Caesarea, and beds improvised of loose straw and flagstones afforded them scanty rest and ample reason for grumbling. While not on active patrol in the city, they spent most of their time, out of earshot of the captain, complaining. Dislike of police duty in Jerusalem during the Jewish feast exaggerated their recollections of the pleasures of seaside detail from which the Passover festival had temporarily removed them.

The Raven discovered that his nearest neighbor, a youth newly recruited to the legion, still slept heavily. Jealous of the reprieve the lad's weariness had won from the early sun, he tickled the sleeper's nose maliciously with a straw, and smiled at the convulsive reflex. It was harmless fun and he kept repeating it until his victim brushed awkwardly at the annoyance and turned over. As the sunlight fell upon him, he tightened his eyelids defensively, covered his eyes with the pit of his elbow and settled again into steady, rhythmic breath-

3

ing. The Raven surveyed the supine form contemptuously and then observed that one unsandaled foot protruded beyond the disordered blanket covering his legs. He grinned mischievously, picked up his broad sword, and drawing it slowly from the scabbard, smote a resounding whack with its flat side against the sole of the exposed foot. There was a howl of surprise and anger from its injured owner but it was drowned in the noisy laughter of the other men who, having seen the maneuvers of the Raven, were waiting gleefully the shocked awakening.

"You dirty . . ."

"Get up, Carrion," croaked the Raven, laughing. "See what day it is? Here we have a holiday, and you snore for its observance."

The recruit rubbed his foot ruefully and blinked in the direction his tormentor was pointing. Across the wide courtyard, on the opposite wall hung the calendar for the day, suspended there at the break of dawn by the adjutant's orderly. He read the large angular Roman initials:

PRID NON APR MEGALENSIS [1]

Ludi Megalensis was the greatest of the Roman holidays, the birthday of Cybele, *Magna Deum Mater,* Great Mother of the gods. Wherever citizens of the empire met on that day they saluted each other in her name. In 204 B.C. as an aid in the war against Hannibal, worship of this phallic goddess had been instituted in Rome. She was said to have come from central Asia Minor and was believed to dwell in a huge black meteorite which had been brought to Rome with an extravagant display of pomp and devotion. The festival was elaborately celebrated with games for and by the populace, and amphitheater and street were filled with rioters from sunup until far into the night. The captive enemies of the empire

[1] Pridie Nonas Apriles. The day before the nones of April—April 4th.

were saved from one year's end to the other for that day to die in hopeless combat with wild beasts or gladiators in the arena; and the blood lust of thousands of excited spectators from Spain to the Indus was sated with the magnificence of the holiday's slaughterings.

To others the day was hardly less bloody, though their observance was an act of pious worship. Initiates into the cult of Cybele received their ceremonial bath that day, a gruesome affusion of the blood of a bull, slain over a grating beneath which the novitiate crouched to receive the cleansing cataract, and from which he emerged, sticky with dark clots as a testimony to his devotion to Magna Mater. So whether it was a day of sport or of sanctification, it was for all a day of blood.

Other eyes in the court had responded to the Raven's sharp command and blinked at the notice. It was not easy to keep two calendars in their heads, and since they were compelled to live under the Hebrew order of days while in the holy city, they passed up their Roman holidays with little ceremony. In Caesarea there would be games in the circus, but nowhere in or about Jerusalem was there a place for heathen celebrations. A few of the Jewish leaders who endlessly curried favor with Roman officials affected interest in some of their feast days, but now it was the Passover, and no Roman day could dispute with the people of Israel the prior claims of that feast. Moreover, the Jews were not a sporting folk; their games were gentle and for children. They were revolted by blood shed to amuse the crowds, for bloodletting was to them solely a symbol of birth or of expiation.

"Why should we not keep *Megalesia*?" The voice was the Raven's raised to a strident pitch. "Did I not win a chaplet once in Rome before Great Julius? It was thirty years ago. Have I told you how the wild thrust of a frightened jackal cost me this tooth?" He spread wide his lips and put the tip of the third finger of his left hand—the thumb and two other

fingers were gone—where a cuspid was lacking; "And this"—
he pointed with another finger at his left eye disfigured by an
ugly white scar across the pupil. He looked comically grotesque
as he posed thus exhibiting his scars, but few of the men
appeared interested. It was an old tale to most of them, repeated on every possible occasion.

"Jackal?" asked the youngster who a moment before had
felt the sting of the broad sword. He had stood up, and was
balancing himself on one foot. "Jackal," he repeated incredulously.

"Aye, a jackal, Carrion," the Raven taunted. "And take
care of your own stinking flesh; there may be others about!"
He laughed at his own jest. "But he was a jackal that stood
on two legs until I cut him down. That day I paid proper
respect to the Great Mother, and the Great Julius paid proper
respect to me." He thumped his thick chest and bellowed in
gusts of raucous laughter.

There was a sound at the gate and as a messenger accompanied by an orderly bearing the ensign of the Procurator
entered, every soldier in the court struggled briskly to his
feet. The Raven was annoyed at the interruption of his
boasting, but years of soldiering brought him by habit to
immediate though aggrieved attention. The messenger unrolled a parchment no wider than his two hands and read in
high staccato tones: APRILIS IV MEGALENSIS ORDER
OF CRIMINAL DEATH TO JESHUA OF NAZARET
STROKES THIRTY NINE BY SCOURGE DEATH BY
CRUCIFIXION PONTIUS PILATE PROCURATOR. He
handed the parchment to his attendant, who in turn handed
him a smaller scroll which he proceeded to intone in his
artificial pitch of voice: "Marius known as the Raven, Master
of the Scourge. Thirty-nine strokes, no more no less. Error by
scourge-master punished by twice the margin of mistake." He
turned sharply and disappeared through the gate.

The Raven grinned broadly but the missing tooth and

sightless eye imparted a mirthless quality to his smile. He was not a little pleased at his appointment, though he had seen many men shrink from applying the lash. And suddenly he realized a singular appropriateness in the coincidence of his proposal to celebrate the feast of Cybele and his appointment as scourge-master. He rubbed his hands together greedily.

"Stand on both your feet, Carrion," he ordered the youth at his side. "Did you never see a taurobolium? Today you shall see one after a new fashion. The Raven will bleed no bull; you shall see him bleed a man." He scratched his stubble chin reflectively and squinted his scarred eye. "And you, Carrion, may have a bath of blood for the Great Mother. Ho, ho," he roared, "the Raven will do her honor again, and you shall become her disciple." He plucked the sleeve of the young guardsman and started to obey the summons of the messenger. No one else moved toward the door; scourgings were routine matters, to be attended to as a duty, not as a spectacle. And as the Raven and his somewhat bewildered companion made their exit he stopped and picked up a handful of loose straws, while the rest of the men indifferently made themselves comfortable again in the sun.

The scourging that preceded the death of condemned felons took place in a small enclosure at the rear of the praetorium. There was only room enough for the guard of six lictors who acted both as witnesses and as precaution against any possible act of violence by the prisoner. The regimental doctor stood by to interfere if the victim seemed likely to die under the lash, and to administer a restorative if needed during the ordeal. When it was over he applied an unguent of camphor oil to staunch the bleeding. The scourge-master was allowed, if he wished, a counter whose duty it was to stand and tell the strokes after they fell. The law that provided that an error must be doubly recompensed, allowed the penalty to be laid on by the counter, or by one of the lictors. The Raven had never been sure of his ability to count. Once before he had failed by two strokes to administer the full thirty-nine, and he had not forgot the four blows applied to his own back by a fellow legionary with whom, as ill-luck would have it, he had quarreled two days previous. It was quick thinking on his part that called the lad out as his aid. He was young, new to the legion and afraid of him. At least so the Raven thought. If an error occurred, the consequences therefore would cause him a minimum of discomfort.

When they reached the court of scourging, the victim had already been trussed up on a post the thickness of his own torso, and as high as his waist. He was bent forward over the post; his hands extended downward and were bound with leather thongs that tightened about his arms above the elbows and his legs above the knees. The Raven and his counter stopped a moment outside the gate.

"Here," said the Raven, "take these straws. They will help you keep count." He extended his hand and thrusting forward his heavy jaw, glared savagely at the lad.

"Can you count?" he asked, suddenly withdrawing his hand.

"Aye."

"How far?"

"To more than an hundred."

"Without straws?"

"Aye, and without fingers." The Raven detected the note of insolence in the words, and raised his maimed hand as if to strike him. The boy did not wince.

"I do not trust you, you impudent swine," he said extending his hand again. "As each stroke falls—and I shall bring blood with each blow; there is no gentleness in this Raven's pecking—after each stroke, break off a length of straw and lay it on the stone, like this." He broke off an inch and stooped and with the heel of his hand brushed clean a spot on the flagstone, and put down the piece of straw. Then he broke off another length, and another, until ten lengths were set in a row before him.

"Make three rows, like that," he said, straightening himself up. "But the fourth row must have only nine. And if you make an error—" he grasped the boy's shoulder with his good hand and spun him around till he faced him—"if you count wrong, Carrion, I'll break your back." He shoved the boy viciously through the gate, and with one long stride, followed him into the enclosure.

The Raven saluted the little company, threw off his tunic, rolled up the sleeves of his leather jacket and took the scourge that was handed him. He could not see the culprit's features. His long dark hair fell in a soft cascade around his head, obscuring his closed eyes and his face darkly flushed by the downrush of blood. The Raven noted the white unblemished firmness of the skin that molded the shoulder and dorsal muscles with a powerful and sinewy grace, and he wondered, for a moment, who he was and what his crime. He waited for the boy to brush a stone clear of dust. The doctor nodded, and the officer in charge lifted his hand as a signal to begin.

He stretched the three lead-tipped thongs to test their elastic strength and took his stance. There was a second of uncomfortable suspense, and then the scourge fell in a whistling circumflex and creased the back with three white lines. He raised his arm for the second blow, the wales reddening with oozing blood. Wh-h-h——tt fell the lash again. The scourger's nostrils dilated and his lips tightened. He noted, after the second blow, that the welts on the white back formed a crude pattern. It looked like the numeral IV. "Four," he muttered, audibly. The boy looked up in surprise. "Two," he corrected. The lictors laughed, and the Raven lunged awkwardly as he struck, off balance, a glancing blow.

After the involuntary convulsion at the first blow, the victim did not move. His body was limp with relaxation; the thongs thumped pitilessly against ribs weirdly resonant, but there was no outcry. The scourger breathed noisily as he cut the air and the reddening flesh. Blood began to run in little trickles down the sides of the whipping post; they started along the shoulders, ran under the armpits, down the arms and into the limp hands. Once the doctor raised his hand and stopped the torment of lead and leather to examine the culprit. He pushed back an eyelid. The man turned his head and looked at him from his awkward, inverted position. He was alive and aware. The blows began again.

But not before the Raven had cast an oblique glance at the straw fragments on the flagstone over which the boy was bending. He had already lost his relish for his job. *Mater Deum Magna* was forgotten; the jest about the taurobolium unrecalled. He had meant to count the strokes himself, but the patterns his blows had cut in the white flesh before they became a confused and bloody laceration, had disturbed his figures. The boy, he feared, might also be confused. So when the doctor had assured himself his patient was still conscious and signaled for continuance, the Raven speeded up the tempo of his rhythmic lashing, stopping less often than was customary to grip more securely the handle of the flagellum. At the end of what he vaguely thought as about thirty strokes he stopped, looked toward the boy, hoping against a fear-born furious hope, that he would descry, beneath his bent figure, three rows of ten short straws each.

He cocked his good eye anxiously, but his vision was blurred. Edging toward the lad, he stepped carelessly into a pool of black blood and slipped, and before he could catch his balance, his foot had left a smear across the spot where the counter's scattered straws had been. He stood up angrily and raised his lash above the boy. The doctor moved toward him, and placing himself between the two, pointed significantly to the victim. The Raven turned. Nine times more he laid the rending whip across the motionless back, the blows whistling with increasing fury as they fell.

"Thirty-nine," he croaked excitedly at the last blow. He was breathing rapidly. "Thirty-nine," he cawed again, pointing inquiringly with the whip to the spot where the boy should have kept the score.

"Forty-two," the lad finally replied, quietly.

"You dog," snarled the scourger. "You kept no count; show me your straws." He stepped toward the boy threateningly.

"Nay," said the lad. "I needed no help to keep the tally; have I not two good eyes and ten good fingers?" The boy was as unabashed by the angry threat as was the centurion in charge who ordered the Raven to stand aside and took from him the bloody lash which trembled in his hand.

A guardsman stepped unceremoniously over to the prisoner and with a deft stroke of his broad sword severed the thongs that held him. Space was cleared by the wall, and he was laid down on a mat of straw with a tunic folded under his face. The doctor, a Greek from Corinth, bent over him and cleaned away the blood with a moist napkin before applying the cooling and healing unguent to his wounds. The fragrance of the camphor oil revived the man, and he opened his eyes weakly and said: "Thank you, friend."

Meanwhile the Raven broke out defiantly, "If I gave him three more than his desert, they were three more than I deserve. Ask that young pig again of his count—" his tone was a whine, as if almost pleading—"to see if he be not repaying me a debt he thinks I owe him."

"Take off your shirt," ordered the officer brusquely. "There is more important business here than listening to your whimpering." And to the lad: "Will you pay his score, or shall I ask another? There are several men here who would be pleased to take your place." By way of answer the boy reached for the whip the officer held.

Two guardsmen were helping the scourged man to his feet. He stood precariously, leaning heavily on the arm of the man on his left. He steadied himself for a moment while the doctor draped his seamless tunic gently over his shoulder. He looked searchingly at the sullen and threatening scourge-master slowly getting out of his leather shirt, and then looked at the whipping post. Straw had already been kicked about its base, covering the stains of blood so newly spattered. His escort of two men began to urge him roughly toward the gate. They were under orders to return him to the praetorium, and were eager to do so. They knew it was not safe for him to see the Raven punished. They feared he might collapse and have to be carried out. Furthermore they were in a hurry to turn him over to their superiors, and get back in time to see the sport with the new victim.

The Raven had already been placed in position over the post. Alternately he cursed the guard and importuned the Great Mother. As Jesus passed him, he turned to the officer and said:

"I know not the laws of Rome, but to do the will of God is my meat, day and night; and his laws are the ways of mercy and forgiveness. Cannot the wounds I suffered through this man's error, be atonement for his sin?"

The Raven straightened himself in astonishment and looked at Jesus. He dropped his jaw, as if about to speak, but the wan smile that met his gaze silenced him.

The centurion laughed gruffly, shook his head, and pointed toward the exit. Jesus felt his arms seized by his escort. They turned and helped him slowly through the gate that swung shut behind them. As they started toward the praetorium he heard over the wall the whistle of a lash and a heavy thud, and the sharp, convulsive cry of a man, torn by pain.

Part Two

THE CROSS AND CRUELTY

Misery loves company; cruelty demands it. One may suffer in solitude, but one rarely tortures alone. Misery is an acceptance of weakness in itself, but cruelty is an assault on weakness in others. There was a time when suffering was thought to be redemptive; we are now come upon days in which cruelty is announced as the agent of salvation.

This is a circumstance that should engage the religious mind with concern as deep as that with which the Cross has been contemplated. The death of Jesus has been thought of as the greatest tragedy of the ages; but its pain has been mitigated by the meanings assigned to it. The scourging of Jesus, however, was, when we reflect on it, gratuitous and cowardly. The Cross has become "glorious" in Christian thought, it is the symbol of a cosmic principle; but can the prelude to Calvary, the scourging, the mock homage, and the humiliation of a condemned and helpless man—can there be anything glorious or cosmic in that? How has it come about that no great work of art has represented the prelude to Calvary and caught the imagination as the Cross has done? Is it that we cannot theologize the flagellum as we have the rood? Life is not alone "bound in shallows and in miseries," it is brutalized by cruelties; and this is a matter with which few who have been oppressed with the tragic sense of life have sufficiently concerned themselves. When, therefore, cruelty is set forth as the savior of a decadent age by those who have become expert in its advocacy and demonstration, the humane mind must find an answer to it.

The scourging of Jesus, we repeat, has been given no

rationale. Unlike his death, which finds its justification in a theological pattern, it evokes in those who contemplate it nothing but revulsion. God, we have argued, planned the Cross or saved it from its element of defeat. But Pilate planned the torture, and a Roman soldier conceived the burlesque, and nothing can save them from appearing hideous and meaningless. This may be the reason why so little has been said about them. The Cross is the mercy of God, the torture was the mercilessness of men. The fact is, we assure ourselves, the Cross has become the symbol of the Christian testimony. *In hoc signo vinces.* But the ugly business in the praetorium cannot be disposed of thus. Had Jesus died under the lash, would the flagellum have been the sign by which we are to conquer?

To the Roman guardsmen, scourging the victim was a part of the ritual of punishment. It was not enough that death should end a criminal's career; death must be made as horrible as possible, and that involved the preliminaries as well as the execution. It may seem strange to us that this was so. We who shrink even from the thought of capital punishment—though a strange perversity still allows it—salve our consciences by a display of kindness as prelude to death. The last wish of the condemned is, within reason, granted. The solace of spiritual counsel, the last meal, the ostentatious sympathy and bravado that wishes luck or confers absolution—these are at polar opposites to the scourging and buffoonery of earlier times. We may explain it as the fruit of a common belief in ultimate forgiveness, and in immortality. This is simply to say that it is the Christian tradition that has modified our penal techniques. And this is only another way of saying that Christianity is responsible for the humane spirit which informs so much of what we call our culture.

And yet it is extraordinary how late in the Christian era this spirit became articulate. Here is a point at which pagan influence persisted far beyond its decline in other aspects of Western culture. Mercy, as Seeley pointed out in *Ecce Homo,* was *the* new idea that Christianity contributed to thought and the new word it brought to language. Plato was not revolted by cruelty as such. Pain was inevitable, therefore the deliberate infliction of pain was often necessitous. Cicero gloated over the overthrow of his enemy by dating a letter "560 days after the Battle Bovillae"—the day on which his enemy Clodius was killed. To heap indignity upon the corpse of one's slain adversary was an excess of valor, not of depravity. Sophocles outraged no audience in his day when he made Agamemnon insult the body of his dead enemy. In so far as cruelty persisted in the Christian era it was regarded as a deposit of Stoicism, it was thought to add something of rigidity to a Christian mood often mistaken to be weakness; and one of the by-products of the philosophizing of the Christian faith in the third to the fifth centuries was the subtle compromise between Christian gentleness and Stoic ruthlessness, to the disparagement of the former. Only thus could dogmatism have become one of the chief qualities of the Christian evangel, and the infliction of penalties for heresy been admissible as consonant with the Christian spirit. Thus, eventually, cruelty could be perverted to Christian ends. In the mind of Torquemada, the simple wisdom of the mouse in Aesop's fable as it was offered the lion, "better no rule than cruel rule," would have been contradicted by Hamlet's rationalization of the murder of Polonius: "I must be cruel, only to be kind. Thus bad begins and worse remains behind."

But not until the eighteenth century did humaneness become explicit in Western culture. It was an aspect of the rise of the democratic spirit, which is essentially tolerant, and therefore humane. The enactment of statutory prevention of cruelty to children, the mentally ill, and animals was marked in the middle of the century; and this temper also so affected the idea of discipline that melioration instead of vengeance became the aim of penology. It is no accident that Christian missions expanded during this period, for the missionary impulse is—whatever its theological presuppositions—fundamentally humanitarian. The quality and aim of preaching was radically changed also. The sadistic evangelism that took unconfessed delight in the sight of sinners in the hands of an angry God was rejected by many who found primary Christian sanctions for a humanitarian gospel concerned with social renovation and change. Theology turned its face from words and phrases and ideas that offended the humane spirit, and a new understanding of the Cross was set forth in language free from the tincture of blood. It was the rising tide of urbanity; the growing wealth of the West made democracy and humaneness easy for its leaders and spokesmen. Cardinal Newman spoke the mind of the age when he said: "It is almost a definition of a gentleman to say he is one who never inflicts pain," although there was much hidden cruelty in his England in which his church was an accomplice.

It is possible to argue either that the humane spirit is the result of democracy or that democracy is the result of the humane spirit. But antecedent to either humaneness or democracy—on the secular level—is a measure of physical security and well-being. Only a religious motivation seeks to transform material dearth into spiritual wealth; it is the occasional saint who shares his poor crust with a beggar. Until he is rendered insensitive by it, the churl's misery drives him to plundering his hapless neighbor. Society in the large, however, sees the growth of the humanitarian spirit when the pressure of economic necessity is lifted. The ratio of gentility to boorishness bears significant relation to the ratio of ease to discomfort. Not that the rich are kind and the poor are cruel. On the contrary! But that aside from a religious motivation, one's economic condition measurably establishes one's state of mind. Those whose lives are little more than the endless payment of the exactions of pain are bound to their fellows by no creative bond. Misery loves company, but it is rarely a creative affection.

This is what leads the modern adversaries of democracy to say that democracy is an artificial luxury for the luxurious, and that dictatorship is primitive, realistic and earthy. However true or false this may be, it is more than mere coincidence that has seen democracy successful under conditions of relative economic well-being, and dictatorship recrudescent where the standard of living has been, for a considerable time, depressed. The moral of this should be obvious to Americans, but it calls for no discussion in this context. What we have called Western civilization has been, by and large, an increase in general education, in humanitarianism, leisure, civility and tolerance. These are spiritual qualities without which our way of life would be meaningless. But we have been confronted of late with a reaffirmation of the prior importance of other qualities. They are called biological as distinguished from spiritual, and include the instinctive ferocity of the predatory animals, the protective caution that is exhibited in the human animal as suspicion and cunning, the grim realism of a struggle for livelihood against natural enemies that rationalizes cruelty as power, and recognizes the law of the jungle as the control of society. "People forget they owe their higher existence . . . to the knowledge and the ruthless application of Nature's brazen laws." This is Blood and Soil as it appears in *Mein Kampf.* It is the revolt against civilization, that, having called Western culture a disease, sets out to cure it by a major operation or by destroying it altogether.

It cannot be honestly denied that physical well-being tends to create moral flaccidity. "Woe unto them that are at ease in Zion." The beatitude conferred upon the poor was no glorification of poverty. It said—and this is a minimum understanding of the famous phrase—that it is sometimes easier to be good when one has neither time nor money for mischief, though such restraints on impulse produce a pale and dispirited sort of rectitude. The essence of the moral problem today may therefore be thus stated: How in a society directed toward the highest physical well-being of all are we to keep and nurture the qualities of spirit that are only won by struggle, and without which society suffers inner decay? We shall return to this in a subsequent chapter.

The recrudescence of cruelty in our time is rationalized by its philosophers as a revolt against spiritual inertia. Rosenberg has written: "We shall breed a new race trained to hardness and cruelty and violence. These supermen will lead the herd of masses. The supermen will be ingenious and treacherous and masterful. On them we shall build a Reich to endure a thousand years." This is no fair justification of the savagery that appalls us, for the corrective of spiritual lassitude is to be found, we believe, in exactly the opposite direction. It is, rather, the operation of a law that we cannot escape. Moral and spiritual weakness can go unchallenged only for so long a time; and the revolt against it is likely to be conceived, instructed, and sustained by brutality. Pendulums have a way of swinging.

But herewith a paradox: this imbruted mind appears both among those at ease in Zion, and those ill at ease outside Zion, but the phenomenon is the same. There has been a rising tide of cruelty in the most comfortable of the democracies. Consider the amazing tactics permitted against labor by those who are economically the most secure.[1] In a more subtle way, we who are not labor spies, "goons," or trigger men share in the continued cruelty that our security allows to the millions of unemployed, whose despair and idleness are a monstrous and unexpiated sin that we must all share. Such things would not be possible in a society where moral sensitiveness was magnetically alive. It happens both when we are satisfied with ourselves, and when we are afraid of others.

[1] The behavior of labor spies at the Dallas plant of the Ford Motor Co. as published in the report of the National Labor Relations Board of the Sixteenth District and reported in *The Nation* of May 4, 1940, under the caption "The Ford Reich" was so appallingly cruel as to be all but incredible.

Cruelty is the child of fear. This is why it is a derivative phenomenon of both well-being and desperation, neither of which conditions is a guarantee against anxiety. The secure are haunted by a fear of loss; the insecure are haunted by a fear of privation. Hence cruelty may be condoned by the well off if it seems to protect their status; and indulged by the dispossessed if it seems to promote theirs. For this reason fascism is always near the surface of any organized society. The haves will seek the protection of absolute power the moment their stake in society is threatened; the have-nots will follow absolute power that promises to improve their lot.

Cruelty is, furthermore, largely a group phenomenon except where it occurs in a psychopath. The individual who tortures on his own impulse is mad or panic-stricken. The organized cruelty of a group can only be deliberate, calculating and ruthless. It can only be sustained when it is organized and it can only be organized around a core of fear. Individual cruelty, born of fear, indulges itself and grows more afraid. Group cruelty, similarly born of fear, sustains itself by the mutuality of its anxiety. This is what was meant when it was said that misery loves company and that cruelty demands it.

To those who today have taken themselves outside the Christian orbit, the cause is somewhat different, but the result is the same, magnified enormously in its vigor and threat. Convinced that the cruelty of victor nations was the psychological result of their complacency in conquest,[2] and that this was one of many signs of their decadence, the modern master of cruelty has arisen. This is no place to detail the ingenuity and terror of his genius; nor is this an effort to simplify the struggle in terms of his cruelty as a reaction against ours. Obviously many more factors, historic and sociological, enter into the confused picture. It is to say, however, that the cruelty complacency permits is answered by the cruelty that

[2] The refusal of the Allies to save the Weimar Republic from economic collapse is interpreted as nothing less than heartlessness.

resentment inspires, and this is true whether the conflict involve persons, groups, nations or culture.

There must be a Christian response to cruelty, wherever and for whatever reasons it occurs. To some, such a question is no less preposterous than irrelevant. There is only one answer to cruelty, we are told: a threat that will constrain or a power that will compel. Given time and preparation we will, under the spur of fear, meet cruelty with cruelty until the terror is destroyed.

It is exactly this circumstance that focuses new interest on the incident in the praetorium. A life such as the members of the Roman legions lived was not conducive to gentle moods. Aside from the subtle and overt ways in which the art of cruelty is inculcated in the profession of arms, their social status as conscripts to serve a proud and rich empire, an empire which while financially solvent under Tiberius was morally insolvent, encouraged them in the exercise of the ancient virtues of blood and soil. Hence the flagellation of an innocent victim was to those who shared it a sort of psychological fillip; they enjoyed it because it gave them a sense of power. This is the theme of *Native Son*[3] in which a tragically frustrated negro experiences a sense of freedom and power only in the commission of a series of murders, the last of which is grotesquely cruel. The mockery of the homage to Jesus, burlesqued as king and saluted and spat on by turns, was nothing less than a refinement of the impulse to cruelty that served to restore somewhat the deflated egoism of the soldiers. It was that animal delight that the cat shows as it plays with a mouse. Jesus, called king by some of his enthusiastic followers, was allowed to play at king for a moment, before being hustled off to die as a criminal.

It is oddly enough of a pattern with the whole episode of the Cross. In a very true way these men, spiritually and economically impoverished, grim and shamelessly cruel, shared his

[3] Richard Wright, Harper & Brothers.

Cross. For however horrible the death by crucifixion was, it could not dramatize the depravity of human cruelty as did the scourging and horseplay. One's moral or theological explanation of Calvary must be therefore made to encompass the praetorium; and in so doing, a fresh interest and understanding of the whole tragic episode may be achieved.

The normal reactions to cruelty are revulsion and fear. When we see one deliberately inflicting needless and undeserved pain on another we are revolted; when we face a possibility of such treatment to ourselves, we are afraid. Each of these reactions tends to distort one's moral perspective. Revulsion exaggerates and focuses the impulse to action, the pugnacious instinct; fear paralyses and scatters the impulse, the fear-flight instinct. Revulsion is also the prelude to rage or anger; as fear is to panic. Hence under the impetus of fury, we justify certain acts as righteous indignation, a phrase that has falsely blessed many a villainy; under the impulse of fear we find excuse for the neglect of duties which, under other circumstances, would be morally congenial. Illustrations of these facts are abundant. Who does not feel stirred to violence at the sight of cruelty; and who, by that same humane urgency, does not run the risk of over-reaching—let us say—the demands of justice or restraint in dealing with it? Revulsion at the violation of Czecho-Slovakia invited appeasement in some —which was called weakness, and a call to arms in others— which was called warmongering. Again it was fear of Hitler that caused the surrender of the Bordeaux government on the one hand, and the brief defiance of the French army in Syria on the other. In each instance we seek a moral justification, no matter how different the cause and the case may be.

In the praetorium we have, of course, no evidence that anyone was revolted by the spectacle, though, as we shall see later, one may infer that the enormity of the outrage finally broke through to consciousness in some minds. Such evidence as we have of fear is elsewhere than in the reactions of Jesus.

One quality of his life of which too little has been made is his fearlessness. In days such as ours, the Christian fellowship might profitably engage itself in a study of his undiscourage-able faith; for it was just *that* that gave body and meaning to his fortitude. The imaginary incident preceding this discussion pictures fear laying stout hands on one of the soldiers—the Raven; but no picture, faithful to what we have come to know of Jesus, could present him as whimpering or crying out in terror. And yet, without revulsion and without fear, he suffered both lash and caricature and by sheer moral and spiritual gentility established in the life of the race a new technique for overcoming cruelty. The cure for cruelty is courage, and courage is the fruitage of the rational mind that cannot be caught off balance.

We have said that cruelty is psychopathic. This is however not wholly true. It is true only to the extent that the irrational is psychopathic, and of course that can be supported only within certain limits previously agreed upon. The emotional (irrational) manifests itself very often as weakness, though it is immensely powerful. Love is whimsically described as sickness; the capitulation to tears is often mistaken for softness when, likely as not, it is the exact opposite. Cruelty as the child of fear partakes of the irrationality of its parent, for fear is instinctive. It is interesting to observe that cruelty as a psychological phenomenon is given only the slightest attention by those who study the normal behavior of the mind. It is reserved for those who are busy with the mentally ill, for if it becomes the pattern of behavior it is due to a phobia that defends itself by abusing others, or—as in the case of the Roman soldiers—it is a sort of consensus of action against boredom or frustration.

And yet, even though cruelty is essentially psychopathic, it can sometimes be cured by the resolute employment of our rational faculties. Fear, which is instinctive, can be cured in two ways: another emotion can take its place ("perfect love casteth out fear" is the way John the Elder put it), or the mind can appraise the factors resulting in fear and dispose of them. This is never easy, but it is possible. There is a story of an ancient monk who one night was confronted in his cell by a frightful clatter and a burning light. As he raised his eyes from his scroll, his whole body tingled with the electric sensation of fear. He was faced by Satan himself. He could not run, nor could he argue. But when the visitor, fixing him with fiery eyes, said: "I am going to eat you," the monk began to reflect on the proposal. Timidly he surveyed his enemy from head to foot. Then he calmly observed: "Horns and hoofs; graminivorous," and resumed reading. Perhaps there are few of us who are capable of such deductive feats in the presence of a threat, but it can be done. And one is allowed to ask if there is any other way by which the cruelty that is a derivative of fear is to be overcome save by a contrary emotion or by a resolute mind. Few things can be of more immediate concern to us today when hysterical fear shivers over the horizon like heat lightning in summer; and the rational and emotional faculties of the masses are being manipulated by panicky and angry men to serve purposes which we profoundly believe threaten the very security of civilization.

It is possible for us, looking back over the centuries, to see that it was courage that overcame cruelty. It was the amazing courage of the early Christians that baffled the official mind of the first three centuries. We can confess that even now, nothing else can convert or cancel it, although it has become a little less than popular to say so, of late. Cruelty cannot overcome cruelty, that we clearly know. If we deny it, we are already under the control of irrational forces. But in the first century it would have been madness to assert that the hand of gentleness was stronger than the fist of torture, that faith and hope and love could put cruelty to flight. By so much as we fear to say so now we can measure the moral distance we have sunk toward first century levels. And yet this truth has always been within reach of the groping mind of the race. The initiatory rites of primitive peoples, that granted status only to the youths who could endure cruel torture without flinching and without protest, is testimony to this profound moral principle. It was no accident that the Indian was called a brave only after such an ordeal was passed. One is not surprised then that Jesus, in his unique way, was initiated into saviorhood through the bitterest pain, from which he did not shrink. "The captain of their salvation made perfect through sufferings" is the way it is put in Hebrews 2:10. Only a monumental courage born of a monumental love, and an unperturbed mind kept his moral perspective clear. One does not care to speculate as to what might have happened on the Cross if he had broken beneath the scourge.

And so, when the Christian fellowship faces the modern world with its renascence of terror, and hears the derisive denials of Christian moral insights by one who could cure decadence with death, what are we to say? And, more to the point, what are we to do? There was no justice in the scourging of Jesus, and there may be as little in the scourging of Poland. But in our present state of mind, is the attitude of Jesus what we shall emulate when we hear the threat or feel the blow fall? Or will no forgiveness fall from our lips, and consequently no redemption flow from our suffering?

Perhaps the first thing to say is what Jesus would have said had he been called upon to explain his great courage in the experience of suffering. He was held by a great faith. It was surely no dream that bemused him. He had lived too long and seen life too realistically to give himself up to a fancy. If fear in him was defeated, it was faith—a sure, practical and rational faith—that did it. Just how sure it was may be realized by remembering that as he began his ministry he is represented as having passed through a period of temptation that would have terrified and turned back an ordinary mortal. That his exodus from life was to be accompanied by terror was not a prospect upon which his faith would shatter. It is not necessary to enter into an analysis of the components of his faith—his assurance of the ultimate good to be achieved by individuals and society, his realization of the possibilities of communion with God, of understanding and brotherhood and the essential unity of mankind, of the chance to share and advance the redemptive purposes at the heart of the Eternal—these all were resources against fear, panic, recrimination and revenge, carried within himself.

But informing all these was a towering confidence in a moral principle which he had endlessly taught and exemplified. If it has drifted to the periphery of our moral experience, we must not think it was not central to his. He believed, somehow, in the fact of suffering as the redemptive core of the universe—as the agency that alone could cure spiritual illness, and restore humanity to fellowship with the divine Father. John the Baptist had announced him as the "Lamb of God that taketh away the sin of the world." Strange figure of speech, that. It is not enough to understand it as a reference to the ancient sacrificial system of the Jews. Why, one must ask, did the Jews set a lamb over against sin? Why not a lion, or Leviathan? Surely sin needed the combative energies of something more threatening than a lamb. And why a lamb slain? A live dog is better than a dead lion, but what can a dead lamb do? Here is the central fact of the redemptive scheme: sin is to be overcome with gentleness—a gentleness as irreproachable as that of a lamb. Alas, that we have substituted the Lion of Judah for the Lamb of God, that we are convinced that only by releasing the lions of our wrath against the cruelty of the world will it be driven to cover or crushed. We have too soon forgot the wisdom of the Seer of Patmos who saw—in a day of unspeakable terror and cruelty—that it was the Lamb slain from the foundation of the world—that's the cosmic setting—who was worthy to receive power, and riches, and wisdom, and might, and honor, and glory, and blessing. No understanding of the unshaken and immeasurable calm of that tortured man is possible, except in terms of this robust and cogent faith.

Perhaps the second thing to do is to insist that the moral flaccidity that has weakened our civilization is not inherent in the spiritual grounds of our culture. It was the Christian movement that established the humane spirit as morally respectable and creative. There is no fatal connection between tolerance and spiritual inertia. To be comfortable does not *of necessity* involve either the loss of kindness or sensitivity, nor does it, *of necessity*, involve the inception of cruelty. If it seems to be thus, it is because of neglect, not of fate. Hitler is as wrong as Nietzsche who is his instructor when he says that "all high culture is based on cruelty," and "of all repulsive old women the quality of Humaneness is the most repulsive, unless it be the other repulsive old woman, Truth," and "love is the collective egotism of the feeble." Love, as Jesus exemplified it, even under the scourger's cynical cruelty, was neither egotism nor feebleness, it was unmeasured power, based on an understanding of the moral energies at work in the universe, according to the purposes of the eternal God.

And if this can be reduced to a moral proposition appropriate to the struggle of the present hour, it would be made to say: the answer to cruelty is courage, a courage grounded in an understanding of and fellowship with God and a love for humanity; and the cure for the moral lassitude that so often accompanies well-being is willingness to suffer in order to bring redemption, economic, political, and moral, to the world.

This is bitter medicine to most of us; indeed it is said to be a dangerous or even suicidal potion in these times. Many of us will remain perversely blind to the lessons of history. Of late we have been told that the World War, in which brutality was exalted on the ground that it would ultimately achieve noble ends, made an indelible impression on the master of

modern Germany; and the morality of cruelty became the
guiding morality of his life. What awaits us when his cruelty
bows to the supercruelty of his enemies? So also one might
have asked on that ancient birthday of Cybele. And yet one
wonders whether the civilization that is to be purged by a
new blood bath at the hands of the new high priest of paganism will survive except it returns to the ideal and example of
the one who, in a Roman garrison and on a Judean hilltop,
dramatized the moral dynamic which God established in order
that we might truly live.

CHAPTER TWO

Part One

SIMON OF CYRENE

Simon of Cyrene sat on a shaded section of the wide stone portico that flanked three sides of his spacious home. It was early March, and the sun was already enlarging its area of occupation on the north veranda as the days moved near the spring solstice. He was a large man, powerfully built and carrying none of the excess weight that sixty years might normally have added to his burden of living. Life in the open, when as a young man he had tended his father's wide fields of sulphium, and groves of date and olive trees, had given him his trim contours, and it was his pride that even after his inherited wealth had brought him slaves to tend acres now his own, he still could shoulder two hundred weight with the ease of a man half his age.

The house, every aspect of which advertised the opulence of its master, was high on a limestone bluff at the eastern edge of the city. Cyrene, rivaled only by Barca as the greatest of the towns of Libya, boasted more than a hundred thousand people. They were an assortment of Greeks, Romans, Jews, and natives from the border of the great desert to the south, and their claim to a unique democratic way of life was based not alone on the history of social and political experiments since Aristoteles, urged thither by the Delphic oracle, had established the first settlement, but also by the free admixture of racial strains. Simon himself exhibited in the deep bronze of his skin, the blood of the Berber maiden who, strangely loved by a devout Hebrew youth, had become his mother. And while the hybrid population of the city showed the qualities of luxury and violence, characteristic of the barbarous peoples

31

south and west of Mount Atlas, there also had developed among them a Hellenic culture of great distinction and influence.

Simon had been studying a scroll. It was rolled up, under his hands, folded listlessly in his lap. His eyes were half-closed as if he were reflecting on something he had just read. In his later years, after the fortune bequeathed him by his father had been greatly enlarged by his own industry and shrewdness, he had applied himself to study. His father, as if to expiate the sin of taking to wife a daughter of the heathen, had taken great pains in the upbringing of his only son in the strict tradition of his forebears, and Simon, in time, had come to be regarded not only as the richest man in the considerable Jewish colony in Cyrene, but the most generous patron of the synagogue, and one of its most pious worshipers. At the same time he had found much interest in the Academy founded three centuries before his time by Aristippus, famed pupil of Socrates. From all over the Roman world, Greek youths still journeyed thither to explore and enrich the wisdom of its founder. Though the fortunes of Greece now depended on the tolerance of Roman overlords, there was still a plausible and vigorous faith in the philosophy of pleasure advocated by the Cyrenaic school, and pride still persisted in the systematic orthodoxy once despised as impious radicalism, and which, moving beyond the critical skepticism of the Sophists, had deduced a single universal aim for all men—the pursuit of pleasure as the meaning of existence.

Simon was startled from his reverie by a footfall near by, and turned his head sharply to the left. His younger son Alexander stopped politely and bowed as he spoke a word of greeting.

"Peace to you, my son," Simon said, in acknowledgment. "Are you not late?" He sat up and looked at the sun.

"Nay, Father," Alexander answered. "I came hither straight

from school. Perhaps you have fallen asleep again, reading the scrolls."

Simon smiled at the gentle rebuke, and confessed that his son was right. Alexander had wasted no time in returning from his last lecture period at the Academy. Indeed he had rather hurried, for the day had brought to him a new idea to share with his father.

"What have you been reading?" the boy asked, standing respectfully in front of him.

"Ecclesiastes, the Preacher."

"Again? And do you still think him able to keep you awake?"

"Not altogether," Simon said, laughing. He unrolled the scroll and read: "Then I considered mirth, because a man hath no better thing than to eat and to drink and to be merry; for that only shall abide with him of his labor all the days of his life which God giveth him under the sun."

There was a moment of silence, then Alexander repeated slowly, "No better thing than to eat . . . for that shall abide . . ."

"Is that not the truth as your master Aristippus saw it?" It was the father's voice resuming. "Have I not told you that Jehovah's wisdom is older than Zeus', and that the preacher taught the life of pleasure before your masters spoke of it?"

"Before Aristippus—yes," the boy answered, "but he lived and taught when Greece was the favorite of the gods. Time changes the teachings of the wise. Does not my father remember it was another Cyrenaic, Hegesias, who denied that pleasure could be real and advocated suicide as the only protection against pain? He taught when Alexander the Great was brutalizing life with his interminable wars of conquest. That would make a difference to the philosopher who must survey life as a whole. And more . . ."

He did not finish his sentence. Rufus, his older brother, appeared around the corner of the house and as soon as he saw the two other men, broke into a noisy clatter about a rise in the price of sulphium that would make the summer crop fetch a fortune even if the olive trees, injured by the winter drouth, should fail. Rufus was like his grandmother in complexion and was a strange contrast to his fairer brother. He loved the open fields as the younger lad loved the Academy and took keen delight in his virile strength, contrasting it invidiously with the philosopher's pallor that marked Alexander's cheek. There was, in fact, not a little studied contempt in his attitude toward his brother, and his irritation at his father's belated interest in the Books of the Law and in the theories of the schoolmasters, betrayed him into speech that at times was little short of disrespectful.

The two men greeted him perfunctorily and waited till he finished his crop forecast. They showed an interest no deeper than their wish to turn the conversation back to its original topic. When he stopped talking, Alexander, looking at his father, said, "That was Hegesias. But today we learned of another who taught a stranger doctrine."

"Hardly stranger than suicide to escape pain," argued his father.

"Aye, sir, stranger than suicide. Anniceris declared that pleasure consists sometimes in self-sacrifice, and that to share the joy or pain of another is the real source of happiness."

"Anniceris; was he one of the great masters?"

"Nay," answered the boy, "he it was who ransomed Master Plato from Dionysius, tyrant of Syracuse, for twenty minas. He won fame first as a charioteer, and later as a philosopher."

"Charioteer," sneered Rufus, "do you think a philosopher could teach you to drive a horse?"

"To share joy or pain," Simon repeated reflectively. Rufus' irritated interruption went unnoticed. His success as master of the estates of his father won indulgence for his sometimes flippant, sometimes acid comments about the amateur philosophers in the family. Nor was he as contemptuous as he liked to appear. Dealing with slaves during the long hours of the day and accepting the hazards of the family investments, he affected the brusque impatience that the man of affairs often exhibits toward those who deal with ideas and the hazards of speculation. At the same time he felt an unconscious pride in them which he would have reluctantly confessed and that was sometimes poorly hidden, even by the petulance of his manner.

"To share joy or pain," Simon said again; "to share joy is surely happiness, but to share pain is sorrow," he commented, after a pause.

"What of self-sacrifice?" asked Alexander.

"It was written by the prophet Isaiah," his father answered, " 'he shall divide the spoil with the strong because he poured out his soul unto death,' and did not Moses say 'if thou wilt forgive their sin . . . and if not, blot me out of thy book.' Such wisdom is older than that of Anniceris, and it is little different from it."

"But is it true?"

"Ah, did I but know. I am rich, but I am not happy—happy, perhaps, but I do not know the deep waters of joy. I have not spared my gifts to the synagogue and none comes to me for alms and goes away empty. But such gifts, while they refresh my soul like an occasional drink from a cool spring, do not sustain me as the streams that flow under the earth nourish roots reaching perpetually downward to draw up perpetual strength."

"But is it not thus that the ancients teach? A coin tossed to a beggar, or a gift to the priest—that is no act of sacrifice for us. Nor do we share the pain of those our alms may bless. Rather do we avoid the pain of their importunity by sending them away with a crust or a coin." It was the boy who was speaking again, and while he talked, his father, as if heedless of the words, stood up unexpectedly. He was suddenly resolved to do something he had long contemplated, but never confessed even to his favorite son.

"I shall go to Jerusalem, to the great feast," he broke out. He stretched himself to his full height, and a deep sigh signaled the end of a struggle that had long stirred in his restless soul.

His son, greatly surprised by the unforeseen turn taken by their conversation, rose respectfully and made no reply, though his impulse to remonstrate was so strong that his father noted his agitation and his parted lips. For several years while he had pursued his studies in the Academy hoping to qualify as a teacher of philosophy, Alexander had shared his ideas with his father. The older man, true to his inherited and carefully nurtured faith, had found, at different times, support and contradiction in the lad's pagan learning; but a love for the independence of the Greek mind and a secret wish to acquire it, had created an inner conflict between the revealed wisdom of Israel and the dialectic of Socrates that would not let him rest. To one who had so long believed the ultimate word of truth to have been once and for all time proclaimed on Sinai, it was disturbing to hear interpretations of life that changed, as he put it once to his astonished son, "with the phases of the moon." But more than intellectual persuasion, he needed an answer to the question that his own household endlessly posed. He was rich. One son was an adept, though amateur philosopher, and the other a slave to the fluctuations of the price of dates and olives. He could not divide clearly for himself his allegiance to ideas and his dependence on money, and his uncertainty in both worlds made him the victim of an acute disquiet that the Books of the Law, the hedonism of the Academy, and the wealth of his acres of sulphium could not assuage. Perhaps there was balm in Gilead, a deeper wisdom than Moses and the prophets, a new apprehension of life that his own people had lately found. He was resolved to go and ask the masters in Jerusalem. He could recompense them well, and would leave a royal legacy to the temple if they could point him to the well from which he might drink the bright waters of joy.

Simon of Cyrene descended from his camel. The sun blazed

in the zenith, and mottled the summit of the Mount of Olives with margins of shadow, thin and sinister. He had ridden twenty-seven days, over the parched caravan route from Libya. The sun had burnished his countenance to a darker hue, but his heart grew light with expectation as he found himself mingling with feastgoers drawing near the city. They were walking, singing, shouting, and the air was bright with yellow dust. Simon too would walk and sing, so, leaving his mount with the slave who had accompanied him, he set out to tramp the remaining furlongs to the great gate of the city. There was no weariness in his step; he was wholly unaware that he was clad in garments of texture and color that contrasted vividly with the peasant costumes of the common road, nor did he notice the looks of disdain and pride and wonder that his striking figure invited from the poor.

Down the slope surged the singing crowd. Beyond them and above, the golden dome of the temple returned the burning stare of the sun, and gave lilt and lyric to the pilgrim voices. There was a small rise to a knoll; it was a round, rocky elevation past which the roadway twisted. An empty cross indicated it to be a place of death, but the cruelties of Roman crosses rested lightly on the hearts of those who, for the moment, were caught in the ecstasy of their greatest holiday.

Another turn, another rise, another song, and they would reach the city gate. But now the crowd moved slowly; many people lined the roadway who did not sing or shout. They seemed to be waiting, in grim and anxious restlessness. And then Simon saw it, and his happiness was turned to bitterness. Out of the great gate a squad of Roman soldiers came marching briskly. They were upon him in a moment and he had only time to press himself into the crowd that lined the approach to the gate, before they thrust themselves past. Behind them came three men, carrying crosses. They stumbled as they staggered, goaded by their convoy to greater speed. The crowd gasped in pity, women pressed hands against lips, white with anger and fear. And then, one of the victims, as he came abreast the bewildered visitor from Libya, fell heavily to one knee. The procession came to a sudden stop. A soldier swore violently. The man swayed as if about to fall. His tunic was black and sticky with blood. Simon stepped forward and caught the heavy crossbeam, lifted it, and steadied the faltering man. A centurion turned and pounding the flagstones with heavy steps came back to where Simon stood. "Carry his cross for him," he ordered sharply. There was a moment of silence. The crowds noted the raiment of the stranger. His was not the common mien. These soldiers—was there any insult they dared not commit, even to an alien? "Forward," the officer shouted, and Simon, with an ease that amazed the anguished onlookers, shouldered the heavy load, and, matching his sure tread with the dragging feet of his tortured companion, retraced the roadway that had the moment before led him, with dancing heart and eager feet toward the city of his fathers.

The man at his side straightened up painfully, but his steps grew firmer. He looked at Simon and said: "You are strong, my friend, but the cross is heavy." Simon was about to reply when a soldier stepped alongside and forbade him to speak. "May I not thank him for sharing my pain?" The words were so softly spoken that Simon was not sure he had heard a voice. The man looked at him. There was admiration and gratitude in his soft, tired eyes. Simon thought he heard words again. "Happiness lies in sharing the joy and pain of another," but he was sure the man had not spoken. The din of the wailing multitude rose like a surge of dark wind. "Pleasure sometimes consists in self-sacrifice." Words formed themselves clearly in Simon's ears, but he could not tell whence they had come.

They were already up the short rise that led to the place of execution. The prisoners breathed heavily, but the escort allowed them no respite from their forced pace. Simon was strangely unconscious of the great weight he was carrying, and when the call to halt brought them to a standstill, he stood, supporting the cross even after the other two victims had let theirs fall heavily to the ground.

"Will you not rest your burden?" This time he was sure the man beside him had spoken, but he did not move. Then he heard himself say, "No, it is not heavy"; and then in a voice so subdued as almost to be inaudible the man said: "My yoke is easy and my burden is light."

Two months after the Passover, Simon arrived home in Cyrene. His sons had awaited him anxiously, and after the first month was past, began to fear for his safety. It was by no means a safe journey to take, and to be captured and held for ransom by a desert tribe was a hazard that all travelers recognized and that all rich men feared. They expected a tale of danger narrowly averted, or even of abduction and escape, when he and his servant hove into sight late one afternoon.

He listened with patient inattention when Rufus told him the staggering price that the precious yield of sulphium had brought, and he showed momentary interest when Alexander announced the arrival of a new master from Athens, a poet as well as a philosopher. In the evening, however, after the dust of the day's long journey had been bathed away, and a meal frugally eaten, and the moon, full to its golden circumference shed its light over the wide balustrade, Simon told his story. There was confidence in his voice, and even laughter. But the strangest thing of all was his proposal to sell his estates. A man named Barnabas of Cyprus, he reported enthusiastically, was one of many who had sold their lands and pooled their properties in a corporate fellowship established in Jerusalem for the extension of a new faith throughout the whole world. "All that believed were together and had all things in common; and they sold their possessions and goods, and parted them to all according as any man had need." This was the meaning of his long delay: Simon had joined the movement.

The three men talked excitedly until the moon was gone and the dawn, red and eager, broke over the eastern promontory. But Alexander and Rufus wondered, when Simon went indoors, if his joy was real, or if it was only a dream, touched with madness.

Part Two

THE CROSS AND WEALTH

Reflections on the role that Simon of Cyrene played in the drama of our Lord's life may be less definitive than diverting. One is reminded of a line in "In Memoriam" in which Tennyson observes that the technique of sorrow is to

> . . . . loosen from the lip
> Short swallow-flights of song that dip
> Their wings in tears, and fly away.

Similarly the scriptural references to Simon and his two sons are so slight as to be no more than swallow flights of fact that dip their wings in fancy and skim away. Mark describes Simon as the father of Alexander and Rufus, a circumstance that had meaning for Mark, and perhaps for those for whom he was writing. One is intrigued by the possibility that Alexander, represented in our episode as a student-philosopher, may have been the man to whom Paul referred in bitter words to his student-friend Timothy. "Certain individuals have scouted the good conscience and thus come to grief over their faith—including Hymenaeus and Alexander, whom I have made over to Satan. That will teach them to stop their blasphemous ongoings" (I Timothy 1:20, Moffatt). Also the warm word of commendation from Paul: "Salute that choice Christian Rufus; also his mother who has been a mother to me" (Romans 16:13, Moffatt) suggests inviting possibilities. That, however, would involve another story and our present concern is with the one already before us.

We return to the suggestion made earlier that the Cross is

concerned with all of life or with none of it. If it embodies or dramatizes a cosmic principle, then its operation is pancosmic; nothing can lie beyond its range. We shall need to be reminded of this from time to time since the tendency has been to segregate the dynamic of the Cross for certain conveniently selected aspects of life. Such a limitation of range diminishes, in our minds, the power of the principle. This insight, so largely lost among us, was central to the mind of Paul. "Christ did not send me to baptize but to preach the gospel. And to preach it with no fine rhetoric, lest the cross of Christ should lose its power." (I Corinthians 1:17, Moffatt). We shall hear from that word again.

The clearest statement that Jesus made about the meaning of the Cross was in the familiar metaphor: "Except a grain of wheat fall into the ground and die, it abideth alone; but if it die it bringeth forth much fruit." To die, in this context, does not mean to suspend the vital processes. It comes nearer meaning to disperse energies to the point even of losing identity in the process of multiplying those energies in new units of power.

> Nothing could touch the little soul
>   Of the grain. It ran to cover,
> And nobody knew in what warm hole
>   It slept till the winter was over,
>
> And early seeds lay cold in the ground.
>   Then, but nobody saw,
> It borrowed back with a sun-white sound
>   And awoke the thaw.[1]

In fact the word *apothnesko* is to be properly translated— when one is acting on one's self—"to renounce." If this be reshaped to meet the requisites of a cosmic principle, it would say that fulfillment involves renunciation. As an ethical principle the statement would run: voluntary self-denial is the

[1] From "Immortal" by Mark Van Doren; *Collected Poems.* Henry Holt.

road to self-realization. "I must decrease, and he must increase" is the first law of pneumodynamics. By this resolution John became, in a critical estimate, the greatest born of woman. Obviously then, in the mind of Jesus, this principle operated everywhere, and had to be voluntarily accepted by men if they were to achieve the fullness of the stature of the sons of God. For him this principle was *crucial*—giving the word its root meaning. The Cross meant a cross for him; and the Cross means something at least analogous to a cross for us.

Now the Cross, if we are right so far, has to do not only with our sins, but also with our successes, and since success is all but unanimously held to be a matter of the acquirement of material things, the Cross principle is pertinent to any understanding of the moral aspects of property. Whether or not Simon of Cyrene was a rich man who followed the lead of Barnabas and joined the early Christian experiment in communal living is of no importance; but the relation of the Cross to property *is* important. Simon shared Jesus' cross in a unique way; and in a similarly unique way, property must somehow share the Cross principle if it is to be redeemed from the evils it has caused in the world.

It is a singular fact that Jesus has not been generally regarded as a poor man who had nothing, as an ascetic who wanted nothing, or as a fanatic who denounced those who were materially comfortable. His words concerning wealth are plainly alien to modern ears, and perhaps hostile to our patterns of thought, but even so, he is as far from Proudhon who said property is theft as he is from Midas who said gold is everything. His concern was that such things as are in our hands for the maintenance of physical well-being should not—to put it negatively—cause us or others to sin, and—to put it positively—should be a means of redemption to us and to others. He spoke no beatitude on poverty. The poor were blessed not by impoverishment, but by the possession of a place in a spiritual fellowship from which many were barred by wealth. "Blessed are the poor for theirs is the kingdom of heaven" is to be understood over against "how hard it is for those that trust in riches to enter the kingdom of heaven." One group was fortunate, the other unfortunate, and to those who ranked fellowship in the kingdom as a primary value, his statements were obvious good sense.

In all candor of speaking it sounds preposterous to say and stupid to believe nowadays that "a man's life does not consist in the abundance of the things he possesses." It smacks of proletarian peevishness to claim that it is harder for a rich man to enter the kingdom than to thread a needle with a rope, but there is no little in our modern world to rebuke our confidence in national wealth. If Jesus' concern was for the state of mind and the quality of life that poverty or wealth induced, he spoke truly; and our distrust of the essential truth of his words springs, perhaps, from our indifference to what poverty and wealth do to the spirit of man. They gravely err who interpret the conversation of Jesus with the rich young ruler as a mandate to all to liquidate their estates and distribute the cash to panhandlers. In this instance as always, Jesus was concerned with a moral problem. The young man announced that in the specified instances of adultery, murder, theft, perjury and honor to parents, he had no conflict. But Jesus, anxious to discover where there was moral tension, tried out the matter of his property. Here was trouble, and rather than resolve the ethical difficulties that his wealth involved, the man went away sorrowful. This was hardly more than a dramatization of a common moral principle: we are not saved (that's what the young ruler professed to want) by escape from moral conflicts, but by overcoming them. The man's money which might have redeemed him, was his doom. Similarly are we to understand the story of the fortunate farmer whose bumper crop burst his barns. He was, in many ways, an estimable sort of fellow. At least he seriously considered what he should do; he was anything but reckless or improvident. And his decision was commendable, so far as it went: he would eat, drink and be merry, which must not be twisted to mean gluttony, inebriety, and debauchery. His difficulty was—and his mistake —that he anticipated no difficulties once he was so established, and therefore set up no reserves against spiritual impoverishment. And so when, on the fateful night the voice said, "These things (food, drink, etc.) want your soul," he was not free to call for spiritual resources against the marauders he had sheltered in his home. His possessions possessed him. This, to Jesus was wholly unnecessary, and so the man's questionable fame rests on his being called Fool. His property, which might have saved him, destroyed him.

At the risk of oversimplification—which is to be preferred to overelaboration—we may say that since Jesus was concerned with a quality of life, he was always on guard against those things that could be mobilized against life. These were not necessarily evil things; they were often good things that, by improper or inadequate use, became the enemy of the best things. We shall point out subsequently that family, and friends, and even formal religion sometimes served man's quest for eternal life rudely. In so far as property was an instrument to be used in the business of living, he was constantly alert to warn his friends against their becoming a tool of a tool! In a word, the problem of modern life similarly is how to wrest the dominance of the world from the wealth of the world. The fabulous riches this globe possesses, instead of being an aid to life-enrichment are fast becoming the doom of life itself.

This is, of course, no exhaustive treatment of the mind of Jesus on the matter of material goods. It is simply an effort to establish the fact that as he viewed his contemporary scene, he saw a vast power that was measurably determinative of all life, and he faced it as one who, seeing a cosmic principle animating all life, sought to bring it vigorously to bear on this immense and irresponsible power. How explicit he was in the plans

which must have anticipated the continuance of his movement we have no way of knowing. Except that his general
understanding of property communicated itself to those who
kept on after his death. The corporate experiment in the early
church, called love-communism, has engaged many writers.
The apparent brevity of the life of the plan, the corruption
and dishonesty it invited, and its abandonment, these have
all been exhaustively treated. What is however important for
our study is the enthusiasm it evoked in the beginning, and
the deposit it left in the Christian mind in subsequent generations. The two foci of Jesus' program were: new individuals
and a new fellowship. Everything that threatened either of
these came under the ban; and because property endangered
both the individual and the fellowship, it was treated—at first
—forthrightly ("none had anything that was his own") and
ultimately with suspicion. "The love of money is the root of
all kinds of evil" came to be an accepted dictum. It was not
a hysterical denunciation of the rich or of money. It was a
simple statement which now, as then, has so much obvious
testimony to support it that it deserves almost the rank and
dignity of an axiom. And so when Paul wrote his Corinthian
friends that "Jesus Christ, rich though he was became poor
for the sake of you, that by his poverty you might become rich"
(II Corinthians 8:9, Moffatt) he was writing what to the
Christian fellowship had become commonplace. Jesus' wealth,
subject to the Cross principle had become an agency of redemption. How otherwise would Paul have dared to defend
himself with the vehemence he displayed in II Corinthians
6:1-10, concluding with a figure of speech in which the Cross
principle was implicit? "Dying but here I am alive, chastened
but not killed, grieved but always glad, a 'pauper,' but the
means of wealth to many, without a penny but possessed of
all" (Moffatt's translation). This language is little different
from that which speaks of a grain of wheat dead, but fructifying to abundant life. It was this sort of thing that laid claim

to the mind of Barnabas and others, and became the inspiration for renunciation of a private economic status in the interest of the kingdom of God, an act that even at this hour is so unconventional as to be almost "a dream, touched with madness." Is it too much to say that it was originally the application of the Cross principle to property that created this new individual and social ideal?

Whatever answer we may give to that question, we must concede that the ideal has wholly disappeared from the life of the world. There may be a few "unwept, unhonored and unsung" followers of St. Francis still wooing Lady Poverty, but they win more pity than honor when they are discovered. Nor is this the place to sketch the decline and disappearance of the ideal that, right or wrong, animated the life of the first Christians. Urged to live, in the first century (Hebrews 13:5), like those among whom it was the fashion not to love money, they seemed somehow to blunt the sharp and dangerous edge of avarice. Doubtless apocalyptic delusions aided them, and perversions in the direction of ascetic and eremite practices compromised the purity of the idea. At the same time they were celestial diameters removed from the Christian mind today that is as pagan as that described by Jesus in Matthew 6:31. Christendom today, in both its branches, is committed to a pagan faith in the omnipotence of gold, and even in the presence of a threat to a world economic order that, win or lose, is bound to effect the financial base on which organized Christianity rests, there is as yet no vocal evidence of willingness to submit ecclesiastical holdings to the jurisdiction of the Cross principle.

Perhaps we have been suckled in a pagan creed too long. It was hardly later than the middle of the second century that interest in Christianity became the sport of philosophers. It inevitably lost its economic relevance, and such powers and resources as it developed fell into the hands of a politico-ecclesiastical combine that called itself the Church. Then came the dark ages, five centuries of unspeakable degradation of morals and philosophy, out of which emerged the feudal society of central Europe. Then there developed a formal piety that the lords cultivated, perhaps through fear and perhaps through shrewdness, but it had little to do with the conditions of the serfs and laid no constraints on the lords' struggle for power.

Protestantism and capitalism appeared concurrently in Europe in the sixteenth century, and flourished in the cities and centers of trade and manufacture. Reaction against conventional Christian immorality produced a desire for soberness and thrift which was encouraged by the revived protestant doctrine of the universal priesthood of believers. Individualism, laissez faire, expansion of trade, industrial revolution, discovery, wealth, rising standards of living, imperialism, foreign missions enormously subsidized and transporting an expensive culture along with its gospel of salvation—these are only a few of the factors in the congeries that spanned the era from the end of the middle ages when "for a thousand years, Europe had witnessed the spectacle of organized communities where the individual profited nothing, the community gained all," to the present hour when the ideal of personal, corporate, ecclesiastical and national prosperity is the dominant moral impulse for living. The power that this puts into human hands is no longer rationalized, but breaks out in demonic and irresponsible manifestations, the apogee of which is war. But until it is violently replaced by another order, capitalism will remain the apotheosis of power.

A part of the critical appraisal of the present hour is a prediction that the imminent fall of our capitalist culture, which is inevitable no matter by whom the war is won, will carry down with it what we have come to call Christianity. Western culture is Christian, we say. Western culture is capitalistic; therefore Christianity is capitalistic, and its displacement will accompany the removal of our economic culture to make way for the new world. It is this sort of reasoning that lends plausibility to the idea that those who in this war, are resisting the breakup of a capitalist economy are also resisting the breakdown of the Christian tradition. From a defense of our money power (called imperialism) we move easily into a holy war to defend our spiritual heritage.

In an atmosphere so emotionally charged as is ours, it is difficult to find a hearing for the Word of the Cross as it applies to our struggles for money power. It is so much easier to relegate the Cross to the business of expiating the sins of our adversaries, or to flee to the Cross for salvation from our own. Fighting the war is sublimated into bearing the cross, and the incalculable horror of pain and blood in combat is equated with the vicarious sufferings of Christ. One dare not disparage the sincerity and the noble heroism that lies back of much of this. It will surely have its reward. But is not the cosmic principle for which the cross of Christ was only one of many symbols to have a more valid application to our difficulty than the suffering of men in deadly combat? We must remember that our Lord dramatized with a grain of wheat the operation of the law of redemption in the field of biology. On the cross he gave another picture of its operation in the moral realm. And wherever there is a voluntary renunciation of power, innate in oneself, in order to achieve fruitfulness in other, no matter how the symbol shapes up, there the principle of the Cross is demonstrated. Recall that in Jesus' figure of speech, the power latent in the grain of wheat was not released until it lost its integrity, until, that is to say, it was diffused in the interest of wider fruition. In the case of wheat, the sower made the choice. Perhaps things would be better off if we were grains of wheat, subject to the caprice of a cosmic sower. Recall also that the man called Fool was so designated because he had failed to provide spiritual resources over against the power his bursting barns had over him. Recall also that the rich young ruler was morally defeated because he refused to join issue with the power that shackled him. In a sense, we in the modern world are a combination of these two men, as opposed to the grain of wheat. Conscious of our wealth, and concerned to preserve it, we are spiritually defenseless against the power that that very wealth exercises over us. It can even mobilize us for a war that may destroy civilization, and we are spiritually impotent to resist. These things, as in the gospel story, are demanding our souls. By a refusal to come to grips with this power that threatens us, we are like the young ruler, morally defeated, for only by joining issue with the powers that seek to dominate us do we gain spiritual power. The fact that he was not tempted to certain forms of unrighteousness gave him no whit of power over the thing that was destroying him. Recall finally that the amazing access of power that filled the early fellowship came, at least in part, from the profound and unshaken willingness of the followers of Jesus to apply the principle of voluntary renunciation for the advantage of others to every aspect of life, even to houses and lands.

This is—or was—lofty idealism. Is there a way in which it can be practically employed at this late date? Few men have been as frequently quoted in recent years as Lord Acton who once, it is alleged, uttered a profound and easily remembered remark. "Power corrupts; absolute power corrupts absolutely." The dominant power in the world today is money power. It comes as near being absolute as any power of which we can have actual knowledge. Is it inevitable that power corrupt? Hardly. The power of God has never been suspected of being corruptive. The Cross, said Paul, is the power of God unto salvation, not unto corruption. Power therefore *may* corrupt, but it is not of the nature of power always to destroy or debase. Moreover we must not be betrayed into the folly of thinking that escape from the corruption of power is to be found by cultivating weakness. Men and nations may be corrupted by power, but what, after all, is the meaning of redemption if it is not the use of power to redeem? There must be a resource for our age, within a spiritual understanding of life, that will transform the corruption of money power, into redemption. Unless we have misread the whole intention of the gospel, the principle of the Cross is exactly that resource.

Power becomes redemptive by a voluntary limitation of itself in favor of the weak. If power is estimated in wealth, then wealth becomes redemptive by voluntary limitation of itself in favor of the poor. This does not involve, as has already been said, a reckless and improvident distribution of what we have to all who clamor for it. Such would not be power; it would be weakness of the most culpable sort. It does mean, however, an attitude toward and use of our material goods that makes possible a willing limitation imposed upon them in order that well-being shall fructify to the advantage of the many. "Except a grain fall into the ground and die it remaineth alone; but if it die, it bringeth forth much fruit."

In the darkness of the present hour it may cast but a feeble light to set forth this principle as a safeguard against the doom that impends because of the corrupting use of the great national wealth of some of the Western nations. We are, at the moment, enormously engrossed in the protection of our power. We are among the *have* nations. Can we save ourselves by seeing to it that our wealth "abideth alone"? It may not be wholly accurate to say this is a war of rival imperialisms; but it is true to say that money power represents so great a segment of the total striving that what we are saying is pertinent to the dispute. How far would the corruption of money power be retarded if the nations could agree to sacrifice a portion of wealth for the advantage, instead of the destruction, of their enemies? We were reparation-minded in 1919. Maybe loans would have averted the present agony.

Individually the application of the Cross principle would make the same demands. What can *we*, as units in society, do to release this redemptive principle into life? Can it be done otherwise than by a greater and greater voluntary yielding of our own goods in order that they may fructify to the advantage of others? Perhaps after all the thing is fairly simple, for it goes back ultimately to the redemptive power of sharing. And what is more elemental in a money economy than the necessity for fluidity? The bane of modern business is the concentration of wealth. We are told that frozen assets must be thawed out by productive enterprises and trickle down into consumers' hands, that business is sluggish because the interference of government makes the risk of such a thaw too great, and that we cannot expect money to be liquid unless the government creates confidence by letting things go. This, of course, has nothing to do with moral attitudes, but it is strangely suggestive of the process by which a grain of wheat alone can fructify. Even so, it should make very little difference to the harvest whether the seed is dropped into the ground by individual initiative or by the government. The results wait on the diffusive action of the planted element.

Of course the world will give this sort of nonsense the shortest shrift. A recent visitor cautioned Americans against the good impulses that are certainly to be stirred by the famine and desolation that already is close upon the heels of war. "You will be feeding the enemy," he said, "if you feed your friends. Don't feed anybody: hold what you have." That is an indication of the spiritual corruption that money power can produce. Nations will still shout about rights, and markets, and colonies. It is an old story. The Cross, twenty centuries ago, was a scandal to Jews and a stumbling block to the Greeks, and we, in matters of the spirit, are hardly wiser than they. But the fact that the world will not heed is no reason for failing endlessly to keep before ourselves the eternal principle by which our money power alone will be redeemed. It must have been an astonishing thing when Barnabas sold his properties in Cyprus and planted the price in the soil of the new fellowship, in the confidence that his wealth would bring forth much fruit. No audit can ever show his investment to have been a bad one. It was to be expected, perhaps, that Ananias, corrupted by his money, would lie about it. That's an old story too. But the word of the Son of Man still stands uncontradicted among the multitudinous and varied redemptive expedients of the children of men. "If a grain of wheat . . . die . . . !" How constantly it must be said, for who knows but that after the horror of this night that is upon us has passed, there will be many who, like Simon in our episode, will hazard money power in terms of the Cross. It may appear like a dream, touched with madness, but to those who know the meaning of the Cross, it will be a further vindication of the wisdom at the heart of the universe.

CHAPTER THREE

PART ONE: WOMEN WHO LAMENTED HIM

PART TWO: THE CROSS AND FAMILY

Part One

WOMEN WHO LAMENTED HIM

Nazareth of Galilee was like many another small village in the great cleft of the Jordan Valley. It had no distinction to boast except that within a radius of forty furlongs most of the joinery throughout the countryside was done in its shops or by its residents. Carpenter booths flanked both sides of the principal street that twisted indecisively from north to south, and all day long the industrious whisper of plane and saw issued from their dim interiors. It was a subdued symphony, more pleasant, the villagers said, than the sharp percussions of the brass workers in Cana, five miles down the valley, and gave rise to the proverb current among the simple folk: the kettle, shaped by a hammer dies before the stool, fashioned by a caress. Such village wisdom, compressed into homely and easily remembered words, comprised no little of the moral instruction that the elders committed to the lads apprenticed to the trade.

Up from the main street, toward the western limit of the low-roofed dwellings was the house of Joseph of the tribe of David. Mary, daughter of the tribe of David, widowed for fourteen years, lived with her family of four, three sons and one daughter. Their house was near the open fields, and easy of access to herdsmen and tillers of the soil, and often, during the day, oxen were to be seen outside the mud wall, waiting for repairs to clevis or shaft, or for the fitting of a new yoke; and an occasional shepherd might be seen testing the heft of a new crook, or sharpening a plow share blunted in the rocky soil of the hillside. The house faced the East, and across the court, the shop, through its very wide door, allowed the amplitude of the western sunlight to lengthen the working day, and a low gate at the south end of the yard afforded entrance and exit to both man and beast. Above it, cut in a wooden slab that swung from a wrought-iron arm, the end of which was bent like a shepherd's crook, one read in neatly cut characters: JOSEPH SON OF JACOB FAMILY OF DAVID.

Since the death of Joseph, Jesus had managed the affairs of the shop, and taught the trade to the three younger sons, James, Simon and Judah. Throughout the countryside the reputation of the sons of Joseph had spread, and their fame rested on two specialties; they made the strongest and lightest yoke that was to be found anywhere, said to have been the invention of the eldest son; and he, furthermore, enjoyed a repute unique among the carpenters of the town as being more expert in repair work than them all. No broken tool, no article of furniture, no shattered staff or yoke but could be restored by him to a condition said to be better even than before the damage occurred. For this reason one end of the shop was most of the time cluttered up with unassorted articles in various states of delapidation, and the other end filled with orderly rows of similar articles so exquisitely repaired that the point of breakage was difficult to discover.

One evening, long after the set of sun a shepherd knocked on the gate and when admitted, exhibited his crook, broken sadly in half. He had struck at a viper, he said, on his way back to the fold. It had been his father's crook and he believed it to have a strange potency which he could not explain, but which made its possible loss all but irreparable. Could the carpenter fix it before the morrow? Judah, for it was he who had answered the knock, showed the broken staff to his elder brother and repeated the shepherd's melancholy tale. Jesus picked up a wick that burned indifferently inside the house, and protecting it with a cupped hand, crossed the yard to the shop. The shepherd followed him, and watched silently while with practiced skill he sawed the broken ends, smoothed them with a crude file, and joined them expertly with a dowel pin.

"You work swiftly and easily, sir," he said appreciatively. "Why, may I ask, do you make so much of repair work and, unlike the men of your craft along the street, so little of articles made new for common use?"

The carpenter vigorously rubbed dark wax over the fresh crack until it was all but invisible in the dim light. "It is easier to make, than to repair," he answered pleasantly. He took the crook by the lower end and struck the ground sharply with the bent elbow. It vibrated with a solid, resilient sound. "And there be few who know the joy of bringing back beauty or strength that has been lost by abuse or carelessness." He handed the stick to the shepherd who tested the repaired break under his bent knee.

"It is stronger than before," he ventured. "What can I do to repay your trouble?"

"Your thanks and your recollection," Jesus answered. And then: "Your sheep drop their lambs in the spring, but they cannot mend the broken leg or repair the wound the thorn bush makes. God has made men according to his own pleasure but in giving his sons the will either to serve him or to flee from him, he cannot repair the evil they do themselves. And who will repair the broken hearts? Are they not few who care? Those that are whole need not a physician, but alas for those who are sick and find no aid." He followed the shepherd to the gate and opened it. The man was no less bewildered by the carpenter's strange talk than by his refusal to ask compensation for his work. He tried to thank him as the gate closed between them in the darkness, and as he made his way down the alleyway, he could be heard thumping the ground with his crook. Jesus stood for a moment and looked up at a cluster of bright stars, and then walked slowly across the yard, and sat down on the doorsill by Judah. There was a long interval of silence. The light still burned in the shop.

Judah got up to go and fetch it, but a draft of cool night air snuffed it suddenly when he was but halfway back to the house. He muttered irritatedly as he stumbled against a yoke beam in the dark.

"How long," he asked finally, "do you think the thanks of shepherds for repairs to their broken crooks will keep this family in bread?" There was annoyance in his tone and it was clear that his question was the resumption of a dispute begun earlier in the evening. "To one responsible for a family such methods may bring food to the soul, but it feeds no bodies." He waited for a reply, but there was none. "Our mother wonders and grieves deeply," he went on, "but she will not complain for love of you. 'Tis well to consider lilies and birds, but not when one hungers for oil and flour."

Jesus stood up. His full height looked immensely tall in the darkness. He looked up at the cluster of burning stars again, and stepped out into the yard. "They that are sick . . ." He started to speak quietly but was interrupted tartly by his brother.

"*They* that are sick, they! What about us who are hungry?"

He moved toward the gate and drew the bar so gently it made no sound, and as he stepped through he breathed deeply of the darkness. Above the village, a short mile from the house, the summit of the ridge smouldered black against the sky. He was careful to make no sound as he closed the gate behind him, and his footsteps, as he turned into a familiar path that led to the crest where he would spend the night in prayer, were only heard by his bewildered and unhappy brother.

He was hardly out of earshot before Judah was in the house again. In the little bedroom of his widowed mother he found Anna his sister. She was talking with Mary. Simon and James had not returned from the market place whither they were accustomed to go after the day's work was done.

"He has gone to the hilltop again," Judah announced bitterly. "It was his answer to my question."

"What question?" Mary asked.

"I asked him again how long we are to live on the thanks he exacts as price for the work we do. The villagers think that business throngs our doors and our shop is full of work, and they predict that we will grow rich and buy out the trade. Little they know that we . . ."

"But do you not fit yokes, and after the Feast of Tabernacles will you not go to work on the magistrate's new house?"

"Aye, but it fetches only enough for meager food and patches on old raiment."

"We have enough," she answered gently, "while we have him."

Judah bit his lip to restrain his anger. "Our father Joseph . . ."

"Your father Joseph was a godly man," she said in rebuke.

He bowed in deference to her words, but his heart was dark with anger and disappointment. Her love for her first-born exceeded that she felt for the others, and such was the proper thing with all pious mothers in Israel. But it was the blindness of her devotion that enraged the younger sons. She listened to his words as though the voice of God spoke in them. Only one thing disturbed the deep of her contentment. Four years previously her older daughter Rebecca had gone to Dimnah as the bride of Joel, son of Elah, who worked about the perfume vats of Magdala. She had borne him two daughters and they filled Mary's cup of joy to overflowing when they came to spend a Sabbath or the new moon at home. But Anna, grown swart and lovely at seventeen, was unwed and the fortunes of the family had so declined that the possible dower for her marriage would bring nothing better than a shepherd or an apprentice to a brass shop. And often she talked with her mother, and wept through the long still hours of the night. The House of Joseph, it was no mean name. Was it not of the lineage of David? Why had it fallen on such ill circumstances that a comely child should fail to have supplied for her a marriage of distinction and comfort? And neighbor tongues wagged in trying endlessly to explain why so busy a family seemed so niggardly toward its lovely daughter. So when Anna wept in her mother's arms, Mary sought betimes to console her by saying that so long as she was unwed, her heart would not be pierced by the sword that always hangs low above the woman who brings a man child to birth.

The soft, bright edge of day had hardly pushed over the eastern ridge when the gate to the House of Joseph opened quietly and a tall figure bent slightly as he entered. His step was elastic and his countenance was as bright as if for the moment he had captured all the radiance of the dawn in his face. Nothing about his manner bespoke an all-night vigil on the mountaintop. He crossed the yard and listened at the door. No one seemed yet to be astir. He went into the shop. On a shelf was a toy he had whittled on in odd hours, a tiny yoke of oxen, hitched to a plow. He blew the dust off it, and put it on the bench as he brushed aside the debris of the previous days' work with his foot. He looked lovingly about the shop—at its dusty walls and shelves, and the little piles of sawdust that he loved to run through his stout fingers. Then he picked up the toy and recrossed the yard to his mother's door. She called his name softly, and he entered her room, and seated himself beside her on the bed. She stroked his face fondly, and noted the tiny wooden oxen in his hand.

"My time has come," he said suddenly. She clutched tightly at her heart and then breathed deeply as if in resignation to a destiny she had long known she could not escape.

"My time is come," he said again, his eyes lighted with an unearthly fire. "My father is moving the hearts of the sons of men. Down in the valley John gathers to him those who need repair, whose hearts are broken with folly, whose bodies are broken with sin. They come from Jerusalem, and from Judea to be baptized, confessing their sins."

He paused and Mary leaned toward him. A look of desperate inquiry burned in her eyes. He stood up and gripped her shoulders at arms' length with his powerful hands, and then held her fiercely against him long and breathlessly. It was the moment of farewell she had dreamed and dreaded, but no word was given her to speak.

At length he said, picking up the little toy again, "I shall stop for a fig and curd at Dimnah. The babes will like this; for several days I have been making it for them." He smiled reflectively, and for a moment the austere mood seemed to drop from him. And then with a tenderness his mother was never to forget, he put his arm about her and led her to the door. He raised his hand and pointed down the valley. It was gold and blue in the early light. They walked slowly through the gate and stopped. Once again he pointed down the valley, but neither spoke. Her eyes were bright with tears as he kissed her forehead. Then down the alleyway he strode with strong, confident steps, and as he turned the corner that would lose him from her sight, she raised her hand weakly. He returned her salute boldly and then was gone, never again to be known as the Son of Mary, but henceforth to be called the Son of Man.

During three strange years the house of Mary and the little shop were all but unvisited by him. Galilee was not so large but that reports of him came almost daily to his mother's ears, and even when he was far away in Judea, word of his doings was current on the lips of the multitudes. Hardly half a year had passed before a neighbor woman from along the street came up one afternoon to report what she had heard in her shop. He was traveling, she said, through all of Galilee teaching and curing every kind of disease and infirmity among the people. His fame was spreading through all Syria; sufferers from various diseases and pains—demoniacs, epileptics, paralytics; and he was repairing them. Great crowds were following him, coming from Galilee, Decapolis, Jerusalem, Judea, and even from beyond the Jordan.

Anna, three years older now than when he left, lamented her humiliation less frequently. James had promised her a dowry and a husband after the next Passover, but her hope was of a pallid, lifeless sort. Mary, seizing every word that came to her ears with a frenzied and jealous avidity, purposed in her heart to attend the Passover once again, and promised Anna that she too might go. She recalled the first visit they had made when he was a lad of twelve. Then he had confounded the rulers with his bright and daring mind. Now, some were predicting, he would confound them with a bold seizure of the throne of Herod. It was all very confusing to her, but she hoped that somehow he would declare himself and set her mind free. So, when the time came, she and Anna went up to the feast. The three sons would not go. Their bitterness allowed them no thoughts of festival or holiday.

Mary remembered the song of praise she had sung when she first knew she was to bear a child; but as she and her daughter drew near the great city two days before the Passover's close, she was inexplicably turning over in her mind the words of lamentation she had been taught as a child, the dirge with which the mothers in Israel wept for a mother whose son was about to die: "All her gates are desolate, her priests do sigh; her virgins are afflicted, and she herself is in bitterness." They had seen Jesus thrice during the festival. He was in great agitation when they spoke to him, yet he spoke little of himself; his fears were for his friends. So when about the middle of the morning, as they were wandering through the booths outside the great gate, they did not suspect the meaning of a stir that suddenly pushed them aside, as a convoy of Roman soldiers tramped past. But the other women near at hand raised a strange and piercing cry. The two from Nazareth stood transfixed with apprehension and wonder. And then three men, struggling under their crosses, made their way toward them. The cry of the women swelled to a wail of lamentation. One of the culprits fell, but was helped to his feet by a swarthy man in strange raiment. As he stood, erect, stiffly regaining his balance, Anna saw that he was staring almost fiercely at her. His face was dark with trickles of blood, but as she met his gaze, he smiled radiantly. And then, for a terrifying instant, the world seemed to darken and go spinning downward in a whirling vortex. She clutched at her mother who had dropped to her knees. The wail of the women mounted piteously, and then she heard a voice as soothing and as familiar as the caress of a gliding plane in the carpenter shop in Nazareth. The wailing ceased for a moment, and she tried to take a staggering step in his direction. But his uplifted hand forbade her, and she heard him say: "Daughters of Jerusalem, weep not for me, but weep for yourselves, and for your children. For behold the days are coming in which they shall say, Blessed are the barren and the wombs that never bare and the breasts that never gave suck." The women were quiet. A military order broke the silence like a crack of lightning. Anna felt her knees buckle under her as a great blackness mercifully blotted out the world.

Part Two

The Cross and Family

One of the unsolved puzzles of the life of our Lord is his relation to his family. That our meager records were not designed to be biographies of him is supported by the fact that his human family seems to have deserved such scant recognition. We in a biography-conscious age find clues to greatness or depravity in the long ancestral line that precedes the birth of the subject of research. We are even facetiously told that the most important choice a child can make is that of his grandparents. But in the case of Jesus, his family tree supplies no clues of importance to an understanding of him, and the points at which his kinsfolk appear in the story, tend sometimes to confuse rather than clarify the puzzle. As a result the most that has been done is the canonizing of James, said to have been a brother, and the conferring of such dubious honors as perpetual virginity on his mother, who has sometimes become, in the Roman dogmatic tradition and practice, more venerated than her famous son. The rest of the family are all but unknown.

Perhaps this is due to the fallen state of the once royal house of David, of whom Jesus was descended. Herod, the usurper of the throne, had little to fear from a lineage that had been reduced to the status of workers in wood. Joseph may have proudly kept the record of his descent from the great king through the line of Solomon, but there is no indication that he depended on it to advance the family fortunes, or sought to inculcate in his own sons, a pride that would have been as fruitless as ill-becoming in so humble a home as his.

Of brothers there seem to have been four: James, Joses,

Simon and Judah; of sisters more than one, though no names are given. Several interesting theories have been evolved by a careful study of the gospels and tradition, concerning the actual blood relation that existed between Jesus and the other members of his family. A case has been made for the four brothers as cousins, sons of Alphaeus, the brother of Joseph. He, so the theory goes, died and Joseph, according to Jewish custom, took his widow to wife and adopted her sons as his own. Later, the death of his brother's relict was followed by his espousal of Mary, daughter of Eliachim, of Nazareth. Another theory, based entirely on tradition, suggests that the brothers and sisters were children of a former marriage, and that Jesus was therefore half brother to them, and younger. This is thought to explain their distrust of his extraordinary claims, and their solicitude when they thought him over-zealous in his work. Another theory, perhaps the most generally acceptable, assumes that these other children, born to Joseph and Mary, were all younger than Jesus, and that he was, after the death of Joseph, head of the family. While this explanation is repudiated by those branches of Christendom that seek to maintain a special status for his mother, there is in general slight reluctance to regard him as having been in a very real and close sense a member of a large family, owning brothers and sisters into whose lives he was able to enter, and for whom the feeling of responsibility was in a sense, compensation for his own lack of family, an invaluable touch with "the feeling of our infirmities" about which a later writer was to comment (Hebrews 4:15).

Our concern, however, is not with the theories concerning his family, but with his behavior toward them. This presents a moral problem as puzzling, in its way, as the filial one. The moral quality of one's relation to parent and family was fixed by its inclusion in the Mosaic law. To a pious Jewish lad the obligation to honor father and mother was as pressing as the duty to abjure adultery, theft and perjury. As Paul reflected on it he reminded the Ephesians that this duty alone carried a promise with it. In other words, filial piety had an advantage accruing to it. Jesus, talking with the Pharisees one day, rebuked them sharply for the way in which they tried to exempt themselves from the force of the ancient provision by a display of false piety. "Ye have made void the word of God because of your tradition. Ye hypocrites!" (Matthew 15:16). He who threatened very sparingly, saved his most violent word for the man who cursed his brother. It was he who was in danger of the fires of hell. Not only so; but, as was the case with all of his refinement of the moral obligation, he pressed the meaning of the Fourth Commandment down deep into the motives that inspire all behavior. If it were possible to look behind the door that stands between us and the hidden years of his earthly life, the likelihood is that we could be able to see the most gentle and devoted of sons, expressing the letter of honor in a spirit that gave meaning and beauty to circumstances that in most homes are drab and uninspiring.

And yet there are some incidents in the record that seem to call in question the sincerity of his spoken words. It is recorded that he returned only once to his home in Nazareth after he left to join the movement of John the Baptist. This may or may not be significant, but it is interesting that while Galilee was a small province, three-fourths the size of the state of Delaware, and though he spent much time going back and forth "all over Galilee," he seems not to have felt it necessary to pay frequent visits to his family. Some writers assert that his family moved to Cana, some say to Capernaum, after he left Nazareth, and this may soften somewhat the censure some might wish to pass on his apparent neglect. He is, however, always known as Jesus of Nazareth, an evidence that the village of his early years remained his home until he died. On the occasion of his only recorded visit home (Luke 4:14) he was the victim of an angry repudiation which almost cost him his life, and his comment on the episode indicated that he felt himself without welcome or honor in his home town.

But this would hardly be sufficient excuse for indifference to his family, and less excuse for an attitude that he showed on two occasions, which, to a superficial judgment, must have appeared irritated or even testy. All the synoptists record the visit of his mother and brethren while he was in Capernaum. They had come to urge his return to Nazareth for a period of relaxation and rest, and the surest evidence that he needed a vacation was the manner of his reply to them. He not only declined to grant them the interview they sought; he came very close to a repudiation of them. "Who," he asked, "is my mother, and who are my brethren?" We have made much of this speech, and properly so, for it gives a basis for family that is both elevated and universal; but one may be allowed to wonder what those who knew him and his Nazareth kin thought when he made his extraordinary reply. And still more astonished—or annoyed—must have been the brethren who had come, urged by their mother, to do him a kindness. Is it likely that Mary heard him without bewilderment or dismay when on at least two occasions he rebuked her? "Wist ye not that I must be about my father's business?" means something to us that may have escaped her agitated mind; and, "Woman, what have you to do with me?" (John 2:4, Moffatt) evoked from her no reply to him, but a resigned suggestion to the servants that they do as he ordered.

On another occasion there appears to have been an exchange between him and his brothers which was far from fraternal. He had returned to Galilee because of the design of some Judeans to kill him, and as the Feast of Tabernacles approached, he was confronted by his brothers (John 7:1-6) with the suggestion that he go back to Judea on the pretext of observing the festival. The threat that had directed his return to Galilee was doubtless not unknown to them, and there is something almost sinister in their suggestion that he go back in order "that thy disciples may also behold thy works which thou doest." But the intention behind their proposal was inspired less by a concern for his disciples in Judea than by their hope that he would declare himself openly. "For no man doeth anything in secret," they said, though it is most unlikely that the Judean plot to kill him had been due to works done in secret. "If thou doest these things, manifest thyself to the world." Was this cheap bravado, a desire for publicity, or a dare? The answer may be variously given, but the explanation of the record is simple: "Even his brethren did not believe in him." What suggestions would they have made concerning his return to Judea if they *had* believed on him?

It is not necessary, however, to make a case for a spirit of hostility between his brethren and him, though, under the circumstances it is easy to imagine how such a feeling might have developed. What is conspicuously true is that he said some things that must have disturbed the sense of domestic solidarity and contentment if they ever reached the ears of his kindred in Nazareth. One of the most profound of all his utterances concerns his predicted influence on family life. Nothing could be more unambiguous than the words: "For I came to set a man at variance against his father, and the daughter against her mother, and the daughter-in-law against her mother-in-law; and a man's foes shall be those of his own household." We may pass lightly over the suggestion that he was compelled to this conclusion concerning others because it had already happened to himself. How far his message to the world grew out of his own experience is debatable, though the "authority" he had suggests that much of it was. For the moment our interest lies in the boldness with which a pious son of Israel could see himself in a role from which, by every reason of tradition and law, he should shrink. But even worse than that is the colossal demand that follows. It was one thing to see oneself as the inescapable cause of domestic rift and disaffection, but to provoke it was quite another. "He that loveth father or mother more than me is not worthy of me; and he that loveth son or daughter more than me is not worthy of me" (Matthew 10:34-37). And what of the Lukan version which uses the more violent expression: "If any man cometh unto me and *hateth* not his own father, and mother, etc." (Luke 14:26). We cannot soften the shock of the idea by cushioning the words. "Hate" is the only proper translation of *miseo*. It occurs in our word misanthropist, and such a person, if indeed there be any, must be an odious sort of creature. But one who hates his family is so inhuman and unreal that the word *misopatrian* that might connote him has never even been coined.

There is another circumstance that needs review before we turn in quest of an answer to our puzzle. What of the word from the cross with which Jesus committed his mother into the care of John? Ingenious explanations have sought to deflect the obvious from being established at the center of the story. Jesus, say some, unable to bear the agony of his mother, turned her over to John in order that she might be escorted away from the scene of death. "And from that hour that disciple took her unto his own house" is thought to mean that John immediately took her into the city where tradition says he had a home. Others adduce this word as proof that John, said to have been a half brother, was now established in a new relation to his stepmother. Whether or not these suggestions are right, is it not rather more of a pattern with much that has gone before to assume that Jesus was already aware of the family disintegration that he had caused, and, anxious lest the mother who was perhaps partial to her eldest, might be neglected by the younger sons, sought to guarantee her security by turning her over to one who had more nearly than any of the others of the fellowship, understood and loved him? This, it would appear, is the most obvious, and therefore the most nearly correct understanding.

Here then is our problem: Jesus was brought up under such family influences, in the line of such a fixed social tradition, under the standard of such a great moral law, that we would expect his support of influence, tradition and law with reference to the family ideal to be strict and uncompromising. More than any other single factor, the sense of family—the Children of Israel—had preserved the moral and social integrity of his people. To maintain it was the task to which all religious leaders were committed, and they resisted with fanatical stubbornness any influence from the outside or any corruption from within that they feared might weaken this family cohesion. Jesus, however, seems to have reacted unconventionally, to put it mildly, to the compulsions of this ideal. He did not establish a family of his own, and he acted toward his mother's family in ways disallowed by the sacred law. Had everyone behaved toward mother and brethren as he did, the family code of his people would have been gravely compromised. To be sure we assign reasons for his acts that exculpate him from even the suspicion of unfiliality, but reasons given today were almost certainly not advanced to extenuate his conduct then. Furthermore, while in the interest of fulfilling the moral law he warned against common practices that enabled the hypocrite to evade his obligations to his parents, Jesus, at the same time, set forth demands on his disciples that went to the extreme limit of renunciation of father and mother, brethren and sisters, and houses and lands, in favor of him and his program. Once again we need to remind ourselves that understandings that we have of his intentions were for the most part alien to those on whom his strange demands were pressed. It must have appeared obviously contradictory to them that while reinforcing the obligations of the law, he at the same time canceled them in the interests of his program.

This was not what was expected of a pious Jew in his day; and while we quite properly feel that he elevated and spiritualized the concept of family, lifting it above the ties of blood and place to the level of participation in the will of God as the bond of cohesion, we must not forget that such a spiritualization of the commonplaces of family life was so far beyond the average mind of his time that it must have appeared definitely subversive. That his brothers did not believe in him until his actions were seen in the perspective of their post-resurrection experiences, is not to be wondered at.

And yet, when we are forced to ask whether his ideal for the family was higher or lower than that of his day, we are forced to reply that it was higher. Nothing has shaken our confidence in the sincerity of his proposal to fulfill rather than destroy the law. This must have been spoken with full knowledge of all the implications of the whole law in both the historic and the contemporary context. How then can his words and actions be understood as conferring a higher status on the family?

In the first place he conceived the family of God as higher than the family of Israel. The sons of God were more important than the sons of Abraham. "Not every one that sayeth 'Lord Lord' shall enter . . . but he that doeth the will of my father." Such are born of faith and take precedence over those born of flesh. "Verily I say unto you I have not found so great faith, no, not in Israel. And I say unto you that many shall come from the east and the west, and shall sit down with Abraham, and Isaac, and Jacob, in the kingdom of heaven: but the sons of the kingdom (Israel) shall be cast forth into the outer darkness" (Matthew 8:10-11). This idea accounts somewhat for the apparent mixture of metaphor that occurs in the Lord's Prayer, a mixture that puts the father of a family at the head of a kingdom. "Our Father . . . thy kingdom come." The figure, however, is clarified when we realize that he was projecting the family idea to the unlimited extensions of God's kingdom. No king will displace the father; on the contrary, paternity outranks royalty. Moreover, in this picture of a father-controlled kingdom we have an ideally conceived lineage (children of God) operating in an ideally conceived medium (the kingdom), and thus are supplied perfect heredity in an ideal environment.

In the second place—and more germane perhaps to our discussion—is the application of the Cross principle to the family. We are discovering, in these studies, that Jesus brought this cosmic law to bear on all the units of power in human life. The power of fear as it expresses itself in cruelty is to be redeemed by the Cross; the power of material possessions is to be similarly saved from the corruption that all power risks. The family is another unit of power, and while its corrupting influence is rarely spectacular, it may be, by its very subtlety, inimical to the wider life of humanity. This has not been missed by students of society. The Marxists have seen it, and in the early stages of the Russian experiment sought ruthlessly to excise the family from the body of society for the reason that loyalty to filial and domestic obligations vigorously disputed the claims that the state set forth for itself. But this is hardly the principle of the Cross. Except a grain of wheat fall into the ground and disintegrate, it remains in fruitless isolation, but if it is diffused into the soil, it fructifies abundantly. That is the biology of a grain of wheat as Jesus used it metaphorically to explain the Cross principle. And since this principle must affect all life or none of it, the unit in humanity which we call the family cannot escape its operation if it is to be fruitful in the life of the world.

This is, after all, exactly what we expect the family to do. The family makes life possible; this is its biological function. It makes nurture possible; this is its social function. No more complete frustration is possible than the failure of two people to be diffused into offspring, or, having offspring to refuse to diffuse them into society. Except a unit of society (the family as represented by a minimum of two people) be diffused into the life of the race, it abides alone; but if it is diffused, it brings forth much fruit. The family is no more an end in itself than a grain of wheat is the aggregate of the harvest; and where a family seeks to isolate itself, or any individual member, from society, the penalty society imposes is retributive and ruthless. It abideth alone, and its isolation is its death.

But Jesus was concerned with the ethical impact of this principle on life, and its ethical dynamic lies in the willingness behind the diffusion. From a biological and sociological point of view the family is fortuitous and what happens to it is subject to natural law. But from the ethical point of view it is able to serve an end to which natural law must appear indifferent. Perhaps then it is easier to see the application of the principle upon groups that while analogous to the family do not cohere so intimately because of natural law.

Take, for example, the concept of race. This, upon first glance, finds its cause and explanation in terms of natural law, but as such it presents no moral problem. It is when race becomes a factitious unit within humanity that it becomes troublesome. This has become threateningly manifest in the rise of racism in the past decade. Gaining its most vigorous impetus from anti-Semitism all over Europe and its derivative Blood and Soil in Germany, it has spread ominously across the world. That it is artificial is proved by the specification of blood ratios in determining race identity; that it is morally corrupt is evident by the enormity of its wickedness in its effort to crush all those outside its pale; that it is subtle is manifest by the easy way in which ethically sensitive people can be persuaded that because a man is a Jew or a Negro or a German, he is by that fact alone inferior. If, added to inferiority he appears mischievous, and added to his evil he appears dangerous, it is not difficult, sooner or later, to be convinced that the only proper treatment for him and his ilk is extermination.

Here the light of the Cross principle falls clear and searching. The idea of race that seeks to build up and maintain a racial integrity and inviolability, and eventually a racial isolation—and that means racial dominance if it is to survive—is biologically foolish and morally reprehensible. Except a race fall into the ground of humanity and be diffused, it abides alone! This is not to argue for a fusion of all races in one pigmental mixture. That is a biological matter, and natural laws will have the final say in that area. It is rather to argue for the moral dignity and ethical nobility of the attitude toward one's own race that will make willing and unlimited sacrifice of social, economic, and spiritual isolation in order that the life of humanity may be enriched, and made secure.

This is what redemption would mean to race, in terms of the Cross principle. The direction in which humanity is today headed with its exaggerated and uncompromising racial animosities is certainly not toward redemption. On the contrary!

There are other adventitious groupings that must also come under the law of Christ if we are, as a vast and all-inclusive human family, to be saved. The case of nationalism is similar to that of racism, and claims for itself sanctions as forthright as the apostles of race superiority. And yet the enormous power of national sovereignty as in ideal or fetish is one of the most corrupting elements in the modern world. Here again our only safety in a closely integrated world neighborhood lies in the direction of a diffusion of national integrities into the fructifying soil of humanity. Otherwise each nation remains alone, but alone only long enough to mobilize and consolidate its powers, and then to fall upon its neighbor for some real or alleged violation of its sacred sovereignty. And that way lies not only national sterility but international death. Jesus saw that with a clarity that shocked and outraged his hearers who had boasted that they had a father in Abraham. That, so they thought, conferred some sort of right or impunity upon them.

That God could raise up sons of Abraham from stones was less a claim for God's omnipotence than a deflation of their pride.

What of classes in society, and their redemption? Is it not true that class power is the beginning of social disintegration? How shall a class be redeemed except by the Cross principle? And what of the families within Christendom? How virtuously we maintain and justify their isolation! Dare we call on the Roman Catholic Church to save itself by a diffusal of its power in the body of all faith and a renunciation of its isolated grandeur in the light of the Cross principle? Of course we dare. But what of the proud divisions of Protestantism and the grain of wheat that bears much fruit if it dies!

How many families, as here discussed, have shared his Cross? And since it comes home at least to each of us, we may put the same question to ourselves. What indeed may be the meaning of Jesus' word to the women who lamented him as he staggered toward Golgotha? "Weep not for me; weep for yourselves, and for your children. For behold the days are coming, in which they shall say, Blessed are the barren, and the wombs that never bear and the breasts that never gave suck." Where is there blessing in such an arrest of the normal processes of nature? How was womankind, in his mind, to find fulfillment in a denial of the anguish and triumph of motherhood? Recently the answer has been proposed that a blight of universal barrenness may be the only way of ending war. Only when there are no more children will the family of the world be safe from its own suicidal mania. Only, it has been said, as women deny themselves children, or are stricken with childlessness will the endless fratricide cease. The fact that such a fancy is refuted by the cold laws of nature should not blind us to its moral defensibility. It might even be regarded as a blessing.

In "Psalm for Today" the matter has been put in such a

way as to give fresh point to this strangest of our Lord's
beatitudes.

. . . . .

There are dark stars in heaven, and red stars dying.
And there are youthful suns, and ancient planets.
How often has the drama been repeated and forgotten?

For this the earth flowered and was good a little while.
For this women conceived and bore, for this their labor
Split them with pain. For this their men erected
Temples and towers, and for this, the terrible harvest.

Now in the bitter flowering of grief, the season of dread,
What is their agony when they remember
That once and only once they walk upon the earth, and that
    this journey
That might have been a journey into light
Is now defiled and leads them fiercely nightward
Into the final and corrupting darkness?
How can it be that anything save hate could live
Within the heart that knows its hope outraged, its dream
    defeated?

For this you conceived and bore, women of Europe.
Are you not crying tonight
Against your fertility? Have you not pondered
The fruit of your labor that rots in the field of Flanders?[1]

[1] Ralph Friedrich, *The Saturday Review of Literature*, August, 1940.

CHAPTER FOUR

Part One: Two Malefactors

Part Two: The Cross and the Meaning of Life

Part One

THE MALEFACTORS

The dungeon into which prisoners condemned to death were thrown for safekeeping until the day of execution was a square pit, two stories below the ground level of the praetorium. It was high enough for a man to stand in and wide enough so that the walls on all sides could be touched by one standing in the exact middle. It was reached by a narrow stone stairway and entered through a rectangular windowlike opening two and a half cubits deep, measuring from the ceiling. The distance from the threshold of this "door" to the floor was about as high as the armpits. A slab of stone, thick as a man's hand closed the opening by slipping neatly into a slot between two blocks of stone, and was easily lifted from the stair side. At the top of the stairs a heavy wooden door swung noisily on thick iron hinges, and was fastened securely with an iron hasp and pin. Only by the sounds that whispered faintly through the deep walls could the culprits guess at the time of day. They were visited only when their daily ration of hard bread and sour wine was left on the shelf of the opening, or when one was pulled up and out to die, or another was dropped in for his last vigil in the total darkness of his *ante mortem* grave.

The sounds from above had been without interruption for more than an hour. It was, therefore, something more than an hour since daybreak. Two men in the dungeon stirred restlessly. It would soon be time to eat. One of them got slowly to his feet. He was a giant of a man, and the low ceiling did not allow him to stand fully erect. He felt along the wall until his hand touched the shelf of the opening. He found a partly eaten rind of hard bread that he had put into the corner the day before, out of the reach of rats. He laughed and muttered, "This is my lucky day. How did you miss this?"

His fellow prisoner heard him bite the dry crust, but made no reply. There was a grating sound above. It was the hasp thrown back from the upper door. Presently the door swung heavily open and the sound of footsteps indicated two men were descending the steps. "Food," announced Barabbas, "get up, rat, and feast on dainties fit for a gallows-bird." The other man did not stir. Barabbas hunched himself in front of the opening, and laughed again. "Hungry?" he asked, looking back over his shoulder. But the opaque dark yielded neither sight nor sound. The stone slab tilted slowly up and settled into a groove, leaving the entrance to the pit wide open. A suffused translucence fell on the face of the man and cast a dim light beyond him into the darkness. Two men stood at the foot of the steps.

"Barabbas!" It was the gruff voice of a guard.

"Your slave," answered Barabbas, impertinently. "Bring a salver of sweet-meats for the lad here. He wearies of coarse fare . . ."

"Come out," the guard ordered, reaching his two hands to give him a lift through the opening.

"No dainties?" Barabbas asked when he saw the hands were empty. "Nay, pig," he went on, "this rat will stay holed; he relishes not the talons of the Roman eagle. They are sharp and foul with carrion."

"Out," growled the guard, "I waste no time in this hole. The Procurator orders you released to please the people."

"People," repeated Barabbas incredulously, blinking his watery eyes. He flattened himself on his stomach, reached out for the soldier's hand, and wriggled through the opening, and as he stood up in the dim light he looked down at himself and brushed the front of his tunic with nervous fingers. He dared not believe his ears. The guard, he thought, had come to take him to die, and was having his last grim jest with him. He looked at his tormentor narrowly and stretched to his full height. For a moment the thought of escape intrigued him. And then he saw the guard was unarmed and had brought no shackles for him. The other man who had descended the stairs was standing silently by in the narrow passage. He was heavily bound in chains, and his half-naked body was a pattern of livid scars. The guard, oblivious to the momentary intention of Barabbas was helping the other man down into the cell. Barabbas' violent impulse was arrested by the docility of the other prisoner. He was a young man, and despite his mutilations was powerfully muscled. He made no protest as he slipped through the door, nor was there sullenness or despair written on his face. The guard dropped the stone slab into place and ordered Barabbas to precede him up the steps and out into the court.

In the meantime, the second man in the cell had given no indication of his presence. He little cared whether he ate or not. He had been cruelly beaten, and the painful effort of getting up was poorly compensated by the unpalatable and insufficient food. The newcomer stood still for several minutes as if hoping that he would gradually become accustomed to the blackness and be able to see. But nothing relieved the black impenetrability that pressed upon him. He reached up and touched the moist stones of the ceiling, and then began feeling his way slowly around the walls. His chains clanked weirdly. He had taken only four shuffling steps when his foot touched the body of the other prisoner. The man moved, and the newcomer recoiled. In an instant he had recovered from the sudden start the contact gave him, and reaching down he asked: "Are you alive?"

There was a grunt in response and then, "Alive? Aye, cursed to live. I who wished to live am given death for life so that I cannot die. Mock me not; have I not suffered enough for the sin of being born? If death were only a dastard's crime I would dare it and die but . . ."

"Quiet, my friend, let me sit down beside you. You have not long to live, nor have I. This day may . . ."

"Who are you, and whence come?"

"From Gadara, and they called me Legion."

"Legion?" The other man lifted himself painfully to a sitting position. "Legion? Roman Legion?"

"Nay, a legion of devils."

He laughed mirthlessly.

"Once I could rend such bonds as these." He rattled his chains, and the other man reached out to feel them.

"Here," Legion directed, taking the other's hand. "Feel these scars. For years I was a madman, and lived among the dead. None could bind me, and I cut myself with stones. The dead were happier than I."

"This is a poor time and place to boast your strength. Break them now."

"Nay, I am no longer mad. One day a man from Galilee expelled the devils from me. They entered a herd of swine and were lost in the sea."

"I think you are still mad," the other replied cruelly. "Else what brings you here? None but madmen do the things that bring men here. None, perhaps, but me."

"And you?"

"I am from the hill country beyond Gilgal, born on a starless night, in a cave. My father was a wild and bloody man. All I learned was the way to take travelers unawares, how to find the gold and jewels they concealed, how they squeal for mercy when a dagger pricks their ribs. 'Kite,' they called me. I fell upon my prey like a swooping bird, and left no more trace than the path of an eagle." The man was talking with a fierce, defiant pride. "Kite I was," and then as if taunting himself he said, "Caged kites die."

"How came you here?" Legion asked.

"We set upon a merchant on the Jericho road, two companions and I. His wallet yielded us much riches in pearls. We thought we killed him, and left him for dead. A month later I slipped into Jericho. The word had been passed around that a pearl buyer was at a certain inn. He had been injured, so it was said, and while he could not get about he was on the lookout for good gems. I took the three largest and sought him out. He first recognized his pearls, and then me. Before I could escape I was set upon by a dozen servants. It was a dog of a Samaritan, I learned, who had set the trap. He had picked the man up that day, brought him on to Jericho and, not content to see that he was nursed back to health, determined to rid the road of robbers. I paid dearly for my folly." The Kite could be heard, in the darkness, shifting his position to ease somewhat the pressure on his wounded back. "But I have no regrets, except that life has had little love for me. Jehovah, say the priests, pities us like a father. Bah! My father had no pity for me and scorned it from others."

Legion got up and started feeling his way around the walls again. "Dark, isn't it," he said half-audibly. He felt each stone carefully, and the chains on his wrists and ankles kept up a susurrant clinking as he shuffled across the floor. Once his hands encountered a little trickle of water oozing out between two large stones and he stooped and licked the stone thirstily. It refreshed his dry lips.

"Why the shackles?" asked the Kite, intrigued by the restless sound of the chains. "Do they think you still mad?"

"No," said Legion. "I too have greatly sinned. The man who restored me bade me to go home. But I would not go; they had so grievously treated me when I was a boy that I feared they would flee from me, or tie me up again. So, instead, I went abroad throughout Decapolis, telling the strange thing that had happened to me, and the swine. The people said I was still mad; and the herdsmen who had driven my healer away, drove me away also. Everywhere I went, people feared me for what I had been. The hand of every man was against me. I was like a house, cleansed of one legion of demons, and then occupied by seven legions. I went back to the tombs, and simulating madness, I preyed upon the passers-by again. Only this time I did not cut myself with stones; I smeared the juice of roots and berries over me. I was fascinated by the terror in the eyes of my victims. I was worse than a beast to them. Woe is unto me for those I despoiled. It is just that I should be here."

He had gone completely around the little cell and bumped into the other man again before he stopped talking. The contact seemed to arouse the Kite. He remarked gruffly, "Just! Who is to say it? Did not the swineherd despoil the buyers of meat, and did they not sin in tending an unclean thing? Just; who is to decide it?"

Before there was time for an answer, both men heard the rattle of the iron hasp again, and the outer door swinging heavily on its noisy hinges. Hob-nailed boots clumped down the steps, and the stone slab over their opening lifted, allowing a wedge of light along the bottom that widened until the rectangle was a solid oblong of daylight. Through the door at the top of the steps the sun was focused as if in an effort to flood the dark hole with a moment of glory. The condemned men had risen and stood shoulder to shoulder, their elbows resting on the shelflike threshold, and as the light broke into their faces, they turned them sharply aside to parry the thrust of the sun.

"Hard bread and sour wine," the Kite said. "By the beard of Abraham, I swear my back is hotter than Tophet! What would I give for a bath of camphor oil!"

He looked up the stairway and saw three other guardsmen standing outside in the line of the sun. One of them had shackles in his hands, and the other two were armed with broad swords. The officer who had removed the slab called out the names of the two men. They could hear the stiff crackle of the parchment scroll he unrolled as he read the sentence and the hour of their death. The former they had heard, and no hope of reprieve had followed them into their cell. The Kite had been there three days, Legion less than an hour, but they were appointed to die together.

The Kite, expecting food, was angered when he saw none handed down, and shouted an obscene epithet at the officer. He was noisy with rage, and perhaps fear, but the officer shouted back: "Come out here, you dirty rat. You'll have food enough all right, and wine enough to make you drunk. We'll soak you in wine lest you poison the birds that will pick your bones."

Legion put out his hand and was helped through the opening first, and the Kite was not slow to follow, but his mood was little chastened as he was turned over to the guardsman at the door who held him while the shackles were locked on his wrists. Legion, already heavily bound, stood quietly aside, breathing deep of the golden morning air, and as the two men fell in between their escort and started toward the praetorium gate, he said pleasantly to his companion in misery: "Does not the Kite love the sun? And who is he that, having seen the light, can love the dark?"

Outside the praetorium gate they found a multitude of men and women milling excitedly about in the streets. The two men, scheduled for crucifixion at the place of death outside the city were little concerned with the behavior of the people, except that they seemed to be coming from the direction of Pilate's balustrade, and were keeping up a rhythmic chanting that was demanding the crucifixion of one whose name they did not recall. But there was more urgent business than observing the antics of a holiday mob, and the convoy of soldiers surrounded the men and began the march to the place of death. Each of the men had shouldered a Roman cross for in spite of the lacerations on their backs, the soldiers refused either to impress others or lend aid themselves in carrying them. The Kite snarled fruitlessly, and protested with a convulsive wince when the crossbar was laid heavily across the back of his neck, but the other man had no complaint to make. They had gone only a few steps when another group of soldiers turned out of the praetorium court, escorting a third criminal. They fell in the line of procession and with the vanguard clearing the way through the disorderly crowds, the cavalcade had soon passed through the city gate.

It was at a point just outside the city wall that an unexpected accident occurred that halted the procession for a moment. The third criminal tripped and nearly fell, and as he was supported by a man from the crowd who lifted his cross above him, Legion, stopping with the convoy, looked up, and to his great amazement saw a legend fastened to the crossbar which read: Jesus of Nazareth, King of the Jews. He had not seen the face of the third man as he joined the parade, but as he struggled to his feet, Jesus turned and looked at the multitude. Legion had a fleeting look at the man. He was wearing a chaplet woven of *sidr* brambles, his face was drawn with weariness and soiled with blood, but there was no mistaking who he was. A strange elation filled Legion's spirit; inexplicably his own cross seemed to lose its weight, and in spite of his heavy shackles, his step had the spring and steadiness of a youth. He wanted to move up in line that he might speak to him, but he could not jostle himself and his cross out of the position the guardsmen held for him. He did call out to the Kite who stumbled along unsteadily just ahead of him in the effort to explain who the third man was. But his voice was lost in the general din, and the Kite was having troubles enough of his own without listening to the complaint of his half-mad fellow sufferer. It would not be long before his miserable life would be done, and expiation for the sins he had never admitted would soon be made. It was getting dark;

a storm was blowing out of the west giving midday the unnatural aspect of twilight.

How long they had been hanging between the hostile earth and the pitiless sky, none of the three sufferers knew. Their bodies seemed to draw off and absorb the multifarious pain of the world, and refining it into a probing anguish, to quicken every aching nerve and tissue with exquisite and remorseless torment. But no word had been spoken save the oath with which the Kite responded to the hammer stroke that drove the nail through his first palm at one blow. When however he observed later, out of the corner of a bloodshot eye, some action among the guard that he feared was preliminary to the final spear thrust, he was swept by a tumult of desperation. Turning his head wildly, and glaring hideously at the man on the middle cross he shrieked: "Save yourself, and us."

There was a moment of dark and brooding silence. Even the rising wind seemed to be still as the other victim said in reply: "Do you not fear God, seeing you are under the same condemnation? And we indeed justly condemned, for we receive the due reward of our deeds. But this man has done nothing wrong."

And then, turning his face toward the man who once before had brought clarity to his tortured mind, he said: "Jesus, remember me when you come into your kingdom."

And Jesus said: "Truly I tell you, today you will be with me in paradise."

Part Two

THE CROSS AND THE MEANING OF LIFE

One of the qualities of the gospel record which is easy to lose sight of is its drama. Man has always dramatized himself in his failures and in his successes and in his joys and in his sorrows, and for this reason all the great literature of the race is dramatic. It is an evidence of the eternal child in us, the spirit that refuses to grow up, that engages the imagination with a tale in order to escape the terrifying or to elevate the sordid. Sometimes it is one's self who is hero or villain, sometimes another; sometimes it is fate that we flee, sometimes it is destiny that another deflects. That Jesus told his friends that becoming as a little child was prerequisite to entrance into the kingdom of heaven was, from our present viewpoint, no more than saying that unless one could dramatize the kingdom, fill the imagination with the pictures of action and climax, one did not enter therein. That he himself had this faculty and cultivated it is perhaps one reason for his predicating its need in others. The story of his temptation is profoundly dramatic and he doubtless recounted it often to enraptured listeners. To see, as he saw, a circle of wild beasts about him, to feel as he felt the hunger and the loneliness of a desert, to hear as he heard the ingratiating voice of an evil one urging him to make bread of a stone—except we are moved by the surge of the first of those three acts of the wilderness struggle, we cannot know what sin is. And that imagined swoop from temple pinnacle to the pavement of the court, borne up by angels; and the panorama of the world seen from an exceeding high mountain and the itch to possess, and the offer of it! There is not a dull line in the play, nor—as the dramatic critics used to say before sophistication sneered sentiment out of the theater—nor was there a dry eye in the house when the last curtain fell.

One might go on and point out the intuitions that in dramatic form stirred the soul of the Lord. Sometimes in a prayer: "Thou hast revealed them unto babes"; sometimes on a stage as wide as the sky: "I beheld Satan as lightning falling from heaven"; and sometimes as a sense of incredible and invincible power: "twelve legions of angels," mobilized and at attention in an ambuscade of darkness. This is far from saying that the record that engages us is fabrication. It is, on the contrary, to say that because of the tradition of literalness with which the New Testament has been obscured, we have largely missed its true inspiration. Much of the record is ours because of the dramatic quality of incidents that witnesses would not ever forget. They would never have retained the vividness and vibrancy of its hero, had they been forced to read about him in a book, every word of which they had been cautioned to believe was eternally and literally and inviolably true. It is we who, losing the proximity of the dramatic to the remoteness of a theory of inspiration, have also lost something, if not indeed everything, of the true understanding of what inspiration is. One wonders whether one has any more right to speak authoritatively on inspiration without having experienced it, than on forgiveness without having known it. Except we turn again and become as little children, we cannot understand the ultimate meaning of life. To a degree which we are not yet fully aware, theology has reduced drama to rubric and thus taken from us the child eye, and put in its place the eye of an old man.

The record of the crucifixion is an excellent illustration both of the dramatic quality of an episode, and the way in which it has been smudged by the fingerprints of the theologians. Our concern for the present is the scene in which three figures, contorted on low Roman crosses, are seen against a backdrop of heavy clouds. It is fitting that nature should appear involved in an effort to blot out this picture of man's inhumanity to man; it is also proper that the effort should fail to obliterate a circumstance that has always fouled the skylines of the world. The three men are conspicuously different. The one in the center has for some time been the object of the crowd's attention, to such an extent indeed that the two men on either side of him have been all but unnoticed. He is identified, both as to name and home, by a legend tacked above his head. This was no more than the others perhaps had, for it was customary to identify criminals thus. But he had been given an extraordinary title: "King of the Jews." This was a crude jest. He had confessed to his name and his home, but when asked concerning his pretentions to the throne had replied that his kingdom was not of this world. He was, by his own testimony, the king of Truth. Rehoboam was the last real king of the united sons of Abraham. Since his short reign, the kingdom had been divided, and conquered, and largely scattered. Few could have taken seriously the claims of a new pretender, even of the line of David. Nor had they. On the contrary, some of the people seemed to take cruel delight in making fun of him and the title which he had disavowed during his trial. But during this onslaught of cowardly and gratuitous insult, the victim had neither rebuked nor disputed them, and they had finally given up taunting him. He had spoken two or three times but those who heard him could not make out exactly what he had said. One man had challenged him as king of *Israel*, to come down from the cross. The man was evidently a Judean and, since Jesus was from Galilee— despised by the Judeans—his title as king of the *Jews* was derided and in the same breath Israel was taunted with having such a ruler. It was an interesting disclosure of the narrow and fatal provincialism that existed even within the restricted limits of Palestine.

The man who was dying on the cross to the left of center,

was apparently possessed of great physical strength. From the moment he emerged from the praetorium, his mouth had poured forth an uninterrupted stream of braggadocio and obscenity, and he had carried his heavy cross as lightly as if it had been a bundle of faggots. When he came to the top of Skull Hill and was ordered to put down his cross, he had hurled it down so violently that the crosspiece was jarred loose. While the soldiers repaired it, he jeered at them, boasting his own strength and laughing savagely at the fragile instrument on which he was to die.

The people were diverted by his noise and even applauded the struggle he put up when he was nailed to his cross. Despite his shackles, he was able to show plenty of fight, and before his arms were bound by willow withes to the crossbar preliminary to driving the nails through the palms, he had bloodied the face of two of his executioners. They had to drive the first nail through a tightly clenched fist. He was driving as hard a bargain with death as he had driven with life. For an hour he railed at the crowd, seeking to draw attention away from the silent man to his right. Finally his terrible boldness gave way to whining. The agony of his torn flesh swept over him in waves of pain, and when the crowds began calling on Jesus to save himself, into the tortured consciousness drifted the wild hope of escape or reprieve. He had known before of release being granted to dying men because of their sheer will to overcome their torture. Sometimes criminals tried to propitiate their executioners by heaping calumny upon a political prisoner. It was a desperate hope, but worth a try. He turned his face, black with blood and fury, and added his threat to those of the crowd, and a foolish demand that he be released from the fate that had always, since his earliest recollections, remorselessly pursued him.

The third man presented another picture. He had fairly well lived up to the traditional expectations of the crowd as he made his way toward the place of death, but he put little heart into his demonstration. Before they were ten furlongs outside the Damascus gate, he saw that his fellow malefactor was a better performer than he could be, so he gave up shouting except when he was directly insulted. Even then he somehow felt the futility and insincerity of bravura in the face of death. Furthermore, deeply in his consciousness lay a realization of the justice of the position in which he was caught. It had never occurred to him to question the validity of the law that demanded a life for a life; and to defy it, once one had deserved it, was an act of impiety from which he vaguely and instinctively recoiled. He had deliberately chosen the life that he had lived. It was no mad flight from a fate that hounded him. He knew the law and had flouted it, and there were times when he loathed himself for it. But once committed to lawlessness he had found it hard to change. Men would not believe him when he spoke of his wish to live after the law, nor would they readily forgive him the evil he had done. Nor could he expect it to be otherwise. Perhaps, he darkly thought, had positions been reversed, he too would have set a bar against the return of the prodigal to the father's house. Most people he had observed, sought to prove their rectitude by a display of their sense of horror when they encountered evil. Moses set before the children of Israel a blessing and a curse. It was theirs to choose. He had made his choice, and would therefore not whine that the curse was on him.

Consequently, during the hours before he died, he waited in grim and unprotesting silence for the coming of death. At times he reproached himself, but this mood passed as quickly as it came. Pain took care of that. Most of the time he watched the silent sufferer beside him. The moment after all three of them had been lifted on their crosses and dropped into the shallow pits that held them upright, this man had closed his eyes tightly. Apparently it was a reflexive response to the paroxysm of pain, but the moment it was past, he began to talk in a clear, unshaken voice. It sounded like a prayer. The men who had completed the first act of the killing had stepped back and were surveying their work. "Father forgive them, for they know not what they do." They looked up and saw the man on the center cross was talking. The sensation this caused could have been no more striking than if he had taken wings and flown away. The soldiers looked at each other in surprise. The malefactor on the left swore obscenely as if trying to cancel the prayer with a curse. The other sufferer riveted the central figure with a look of incredulity and hope.

The aim of the dramatist is to say something about life. It may be cynical, flippant, scornful or servile, but the great dramatists have always seen life as something great; great in its triumph or in its tragedy, great in its pathos or in its humor. In the passage of genuine eloquence with which Walter Lippmann closed his widely read *Preface to Morals*, he describes the way in which "the mature man" faces the world. "Since nothing gnawed at his vitals, neither doubt nor ambition, nor frustration, nor fear, he would move easily through life. And so whether he saw the thing as comedy, or high tragedy, or plain farce, he would affirm that it is what it is, and that the wise man can enjoy it."[1] But there is another view of "the mature man," and it is supplied us in the dramatic episode under our survey.

Looking at our story with a view to discovering its dramatic instead of its theological values, we discover at once that in the three characters outlined against the moving background of sky and cloud we have three definite and distinct understandings of life. The man on the left defied life; the man on the right accepted life; the Man in the middle transcended life. Pessimism, realism, idealism they might severally be called; or within a somewhat inexact classification: cynicism, Stoicism, and Christianity. When Prometheus, angered by the fact that caves were cold and nights were dark, and by the

[1] Walter Lippmann, *A Preface to Morals*, Macmillan, p. 330.

endless shivering of naked men and the eating of raw foods, defied the fate that had pursued man with frost and shadow, and stole the lightning from the threatening hand of Zeus, he became, according to the most fascinating of the Greek myths, the greatest benefactor of man. But such defiance of fate could not go unpunished. Zeus therefore chained him to the rocky face of a mountain in the Caucasus, where until rescued by Hercules, his vitals were endlessly torn by a vulture. Just why Hercules, always the assistant of Zeus, on his way back from the capture of the mares of Diomedes, should have remitted the penalty and freed the culprit is not clear, but that there is a relentless gnawing at the vitals of the man who defies life and steals the prerogatives of the gods is too sure a picture of one type of human experience to be missed. That is the way some men live. It is the only approach to misfortune, danger, frustration or folly they can make. Their lives will be a protest against existence, and ere they die, they will curse God. Even the good and the beautiful and the true are distrusted or despised as things that mock man's hopes in a universe that is essentially malign. This is the man on the left.

In a recent novel—it is a grim and cynical story—by one who has written much and well, this confession of the principal character greets one after a single page is turned:

I have loved and I have hated.
Let the ethical people hold up their hands in horror when I confess that successful and triumphant hatred has seemed almost as good to me as love.
I did not turn my other cheek to the enemy. He smote me bitterly and brutally, but when my own hour was ripe I gave back to him with ruthlessness the blows that I had taken.[2]

Here we encounter an advance upon the philosophy of the Defiant. Hate there is in the world, and love also. To be successful as a hater is almost (one wonders a bit at the

---

[2] Warwick Deeping, *Malice of Men*, Alfred Knopf, p. 4.

qualification) as good as successful love. There are enemies to be dealt with, and the manner of dealing is to return brutality for brutality, an eye for an eye. In this case man asks nothing of life except that its balances be struck, its debts paid. If he is shrewd he will keep his own accounts; if he is stupid, life will not cheat him too grossly either of good or ill. Such victory as one wins is not the victory of hatred *over* love, or of love *over* hatred. It is rather triumph *in* hatred, or triumph *in* love.

> In the fell clutch of circumstance
> I have not winced nor cried aloud.
> Under the bludgeonings of chance
> My head is bloody, but unbowed.[3]

This is the man on the right, the "mature man" perhaps, of Lippmann's quotation.

What is to be said of the Man in the middle? To him the universe has meaning, but it is to be found in no such impersonal concept as Fate. The wealth and beauty and power of the natural world did not have to be filched from a niggardly deity before man could make use of them. "And God planted a garden eastward in Eden; and there he put the man whom he had formed." But man's use of the world God had made and pronounced good was to be neither prodigal nor haphazard. More than these gifts of nature were the gifts of the spirit. Wisdom was to be won, beauty was to be created, goodness was to be achieved, and love was to be felt and nourished in the breast. Not all would find these gifts of the spirit in equal abundance. Some would be less than wise, less than lovely, less than good, but this lesser measure was not the evil design of a partial or pretending god. There was a way always open that led up and out to greater understanding, to more ravishing glimpses of beauty, to more godlike levels of behavior. Such a life was not the prisoner of time, such

[3] W. E. Henley, "Invictus," *The World's Great Religious Poetry*, Hill . . . Macmillan.

gifts were not locked against the fumbling touch of even the least of the sons of men. Man who was created out of the dust of the ground was illumined by a spirit within him, the candle of his soul was lit by the fire of God. This was eternal life. It did not cry aloud or lift up its voice in the streets. The feet that walked the hard way, carried the heart that could transform pain into laughter and despair into exultation. This was the Man in the center.

When three such incarnations of life philosophies meet, drama is in the making. The history, both of ethics and philosophy, is simply the record of the dramatic give and take of the spirits that, stirring to action, move men out of the wings, across the vast stage, and into the wings again at last. More than that. The scene that is before us in our modern world and in which we are taking part, is to be understood only in terms of the play and interplay of the spirits of the world. Sometimes the play is an exchange of pleasantries, sometimes it is a contest of fevered and ruthless antagonisms; sometimes the players stand agreed, sometimes they struggle and fall in bitter conflict. But it is these spirits, these varied outlooks on life that make the drama a living and unfolding and eternal thing. "For our wrestling is not against flesh and blood . . . but against the spiritual hosts of wickedness in the heavenly places."[4]

But drama has meaning only in the issue of the struggle. One wearies sooner or later at the passing back and forth of the players if they move aimlessly and arrive nowhere. And while it must be true that those who view life within the limits of finitude cannot see the ultimate denouement, there are incidental sequences and climaxes that occur to cast down or lift up the spectator. In so far as the philosophy one espouses wins, he rejoices; if it loses he either despairs or turns his face in another direction. Here again our episode refreshes us.

[4] Ephesians 6:12.

It seems like a shocking thing that one so unequivocally committed to the eternal values in life and so utterly confident of their ultimate victory should have been the victim of the raillery and insults of grosser spirits. And yet how otherwise was the way of life that was being dramatized on the cross to set the stage for one of its most spectacular victories? None of the three men had anything to ask or to give either of the other two in the desperateness of the situation that held them all. Death hovered on black wings above them, and neither hope nor dereliction could stop the beating of its heavy pinions. For three hours one man had shouted his challenge to death to come and take him if it dared. Another man had faced his own hopelessness, and yielded to the doom that an evenhanded justice had pronounced. But the third man was apparently unperturbed by the prospect of death and wholly unmindful of himself. Only twice during three mad hours had he spoken. He had forgiven those who had spitted him like a carcass, and those who had exhausted every ingenuity of opprobrium while he hung defenseless above them. Later, catching sight of his mother sick with anguish at the edge of the crowd, he had directed a friend to attend to her. What sort of behavior was this? It was not defiance, nor was it acceptance of Fate. Was it not rather the splendor of a new sort of victory over injustice and ignominy, and over the pangs of mortal suffering?

Perhaps it was another effort of life to mock man's impotence. There was a rasping and almost inchoate cry. "If you are the Christ, save thyself and us." It was the last word of desperation, a desperation that will hazard even a word of unfaithfulness to one's own creed of defiance if it will save. But no answer came from the Man who had forgiven those whose work of death was so soon to be over. Instead, from the man on the other side of him came a word of pained remonstrance to one, and of supplication to the other. "We receive the just reward of our sins. Remember me when thou

comest." Was it penitence? Perhaps, in a general sort of way
—a confession of the guilt of both of the malefactors. Was it
a plea for forgiveness by the merit of the cross an impotent
arm's length away? Hardly. Was it not rather—and this is the
drama of it—was it not rather a turning of the mind toward
one who in his mortal dying was bearing witness to the
immortality of his way of life? "Except a grain of wheat fall
into the ground and die . . ." Diffusion even in death,
diffusion in forgiveness, in concern for his mother, and finally,
at the very last, a diffusion of himself into the hands of his
heavenly Father.[5]

Here was a dramatization of the Cross principle in its most
spectacular setting and issue. It is not necessary to speculate
on the strange circumstance that finds a brigand using the
language of Jesus, concerning his coming in his kingdom.
Some there are who affirm him to have been a Zealot, not
unacquainted with Jesus' talk of the kingdom of God, a program he had not consented to support because Jesus planned
to redeem the world by falling into the ground and dying.
This is unimportant to the inherent drama. Of less importance is the use of the episode to "prove" that the mercy of
God can be invoked by the sinner, who, up until the moment
of imminent death has remained obdurate in his sin. The
extreme unction of our Lord was no such formal or frivolous
thing. Of greater interest than either of these two uses of the
story, is the occurrence of the word Paradise. The thief had
asked for remembrance in the kingdom; Jesus promised him
entrance into Paradise—a word that sounds strange on his
lips. Why the promise? Perhaps, as death rolled toward him
like a thick shadow his mind ran over words familiar and

[5] "Those who best promote life do not have life (physical life) for their
purpose. They aim rather at what seems like a gradual incarnation, a
bringing into our human existence of something eternal . . . remote
from the devouring jaws of time." Bertrand Russell in *Why Men Fight*,
pp. 268-269.

comforting, words about green pastures and still waters and the restoration of the soul, of courage and high heart while walking through the shadow. Or perhaps in a flash of recollection there was a glimpse of the Eden every pious Jewish lad must have loved to think about, and of that garden planted to the east, radiant with fruit and flower and lyrical with the voice of birds, where man was to labor and love and live. The land of beginnings, of goodness, of beauty, of truth. What caused his use of the word we shall never know, but it is proper at least to imagine that to this broken man beside him, Paradise was the word that carried the perfect consolation.

So the scene closes. The Defiant, the Accepter, the Transcender of Life, these three. They died a common death on common crosses on a common hill; but it was the Transcender who, to the world that instinctively trusts, wistfully at times and sometimes passionately, in love, in sacrifice, and in God, —it was he who dramatized in death the meaning that lives eternally at the heart of the universe.

CHAPTER FIVE

Part One: Those Who Passed By
Part Two: The Cross and Liberalism

Part One

THOSE WHO PASSED BY

The village of Nain, long since lost in the dust of ancient Galilee, is still held in place in the memory of the years by the frail hands of a nameless widow and her son. Under the shadow of the proud summit of Mount Tabor, refreshed by the fertile and fragrant plain of Esdraelon, and beckoned toward the Great Sea by the white finger of Mount Carmel, the villagers of the simple town spent their indifferent days in shop, field and market, and came home at dusk to rest from their weariness in simple homes. Nain could boast no ancient episode such as gave fame to the neighbor town of Shunem. Jeremiah had once said boldly that the might of Jehovah advancing against the King of Egypt would be as Tabor and Carmel; but though Nain nestled nearest the base of the great mountain, she could claim little celebrity from the prophet's daring words. And so her people passed their lives undisturbed by great hopes, and undismayed by little fears, destined to pass out of time unknown save for the recollection of a casual visit hidden in a desultory record.

Except for one man, perhaps, though his name is also forgot. He was a teacher who nourished the ambition to become some day a great scribe. As a youth he had pored over the sacred books, his mind stirred to restlessness by the hopes and the disappointments of the prophets, and seeing in himself at times the fulfillment of the promises of Jehovah, and even, more recklessly, imagining himself as the agent of the great restitution.

But rewards for his diligence and his dreams came slowly. Teaching the village school was a dispiriting routine. Nothing was asked of him except that the law be laid upon the hearts of the children, and he soon found that when it was applied with too severe pressure, parents threateningly inquired if he was not too zealous for the forms of the ancient tradition, and whether he was trying to make prophets prematurely out of future shopkeepers and vinedressers. He had married in due time, and his bride dutifully shared his enthusiasms, but when their first and only son was born, her hands were filled with new and practical duties, while his head was agitated by new dreams. Thus for ten years life had moved on for them, his visions never dimmed, even by the dull indifference of those with whom he dared to share them, until, partly through a deeply born and long-suppressed anger he cried out one evening in remonstrance to the elders as they sat in the gate when the new moon called them to the solemn council.

He had been asked to make an explanation concerning the discipline in the village school. It was, they complained, too harsh. Moreover, the minds of the older lads were reported to be disturbed by notions that seemed new and dangerous, and were not according to the ancient law. The young teacher dared to ask the grave and threatening men wherein their knowledge of the law was superior to his, and to their angry retort that much of his teaching was nonsense out of his own perverse head, he replied with a passage from Jeremiah which long since he had found to be the solace and hope of his restless mind. "Behold the days will come, saith Jehovah, that I will make a new covenant with the house of Israel, and with the house of Judah: not according to the covenant that I made with their fathers that day I took them by the hand to bring them out of the land of Egypt; which my covenant they broke, although I was a husband unto them, saith Jehovah. But this is the covenant that I will make with the house of Israel after those days, saith Jehovah: I will put my law in their inward parts, and in their heart will I write it; and I shall be their God, and they shall be my people. And they shall teach no more every man his neighbor, saying, Know Jehovah; for they shall all know me, from the least of them to the greatest, saith Jehovah: for I will forgive their iniquity, and their sin will I remember no more."[1]

Despite the authentic sound of the words and the man's insistence that they were Jeremiah's, one of the elders sniffed contemptuously and observed that these were no times for new covenants. His fellows nodded in approval, and another added accusingly, "You show great fondness for those scriptures that encourage your idleness. What else can be the reason for your saying, 'They shall teach no more every man his neighbor'?"

"But it is the word of Jeremiah," answered the teacher, defensively.

"Aye, and what save a dungeon did he get for his folly?" the other answered hotly. "And mayhap you would prefer a dungeon to a schoolroom. You would find vermin there to listen to your tales. But while you sit in the seat of learning in our town, you will henceforth spare us your wisdom and instruct our sons in the ways of God." There was a grunt of unanimous assent to this speech, and the speaker beamed with surprise and delight at his own sudden clarification of the matter.

"But," the teacher continued testily, "I teach the way of God, did you but . . ."

Such an angry outbreak of rebuke greeted his attempt to justify himself that he was silenced by its clamor, and turning angrily from the council, he made his way home in the twilight, his heart heavy with disappointment and apprehension. His apprehensions were justified. It was not long reaching his ears that the elders were seeking a new scribe and had found in the village rabbi a strong supporter of their plan to make a change. The elders were shocked and not a little pleased to

[1] Jeremiah 31:31-34.

learn that teacher and rabbi had many times differed violently, and had the rabbi been anything but a cowardly little conformist, he long ago would have made an issue. His silence was due to his fear of the superior wisdom and zeal of the teacher; but when he found the elders suspicious of what was going on, he eagerly supplied them with much more incriminating material than the school children had hinted at. To the satisfaction of the elders it was established that their village school was under the control of a man who believed in an inner covenant that was perennially renewed in all questing hearts, a covenant which he claimed was more valid than Moses'. This was of course not only foolish, it was dangerous. What would become of the priesthood, the festivals, yes, and even the law itself if such things were allowed? And what about the temple in Jerusalem, and what of the nation? It was impossible to cure a madman of the vertigo of his own dizzy ideas, but that was no reason for putting him in charge of a school. Within a little less than a year, the young dreamer was accordingly relieved of his position. He thought there was a cruel delight sharpening the eyes of the chief of the elders as he came to deliver the official order that had already reached him by gossiping tongues. There were four of the older boys in the school who expressed their outrage and promised to come to him privately for instruction. His own son, still hardly more than a lad, warmed his heart by his loyalty, and, though it had to be rebuked, his childish rage against the old men deeply gratified his father.

The day the news came to him, he took a jug of water, some dried figs and a morsel of bread and climbed to the top of Mount Tabor alone. He stayed there, resting in the cleft of a great rock when the sun was hot, but he did not descend until long after the darkness had laid the towering mountain away to sleep, shrouded in a dark mist. But many times during the day, his eyes rested affectionately on the little village nestled so near its base, and he was surprised to note that the pity that stirred his heart was for its people, and not for himself.

The fortunes of the little family, always precarious, within a year became critical. The teacher held a few of the boys together for a while, but they afforded him no income, and pretty soon they found the odium that attached to his tutelage rather more than they could bear. For a few months after his dismissal he found groups of people in the village willing to listen to him as he expounded his novel ideas in the streets or on market days among the booths; but they soon wearied of his talk. Nevertheless he did not give up his dream, or abate his energy. A journey among nearby villages brought him momentary respite from the dull minds of his neighbors, and he was able to bring home to his family the meager hire his labors commanded. But he stayed only brief intervals at these places, and found that even the shortest stay was followed up by a report, quickly circulated, that he was mildly mad, and perhaps a dangerous person. "Is it nothing to you, all ye that pass by," he would cry as he stood at an intersection, quoting his favorite prophet, but fewer and fewer were those who stopped to heed his words. It was eight years later that he died. Sympathetic neighbors said he died of grief; those who had all along distrusted him gave glory to God for saving their generation from the pestilence of his ideas. His widow, faithful to him, and encouraging his ill-rewarded efforts when all others stood against him, mourned him long and devotedly, and on the day of his burial, in spite of the poverty of his obsequies and the blackness of the future, dedicated herself to tend the flame of his courage and idealism in their son, so that his dauntless piety would not die with his death.

Two years more lightened the burden of her grief by the realization with each passing day of the likeness of her growing son to his dead father. He looked like him, had that eager passion for learning, and the courage and persuasiveness in argument that the villagers, however they had deprecated it in his father, had never been able to forget. His mother, given to works of mercy among the needy, endeared herself by the simplicity and gentleness of her bearing, and there were many who, recalling the injustice of earlier years, sought in subtle ways to expiate it. There was much, indeed, to mitigate the loneliness of the days, and as she thought of the future, she saw her son, entering into the career his father had dreamed of, some day a great teacher perhaps, or even a great ruler among his people.

"Mother," the young man said to her as they finished their evening meal.

"Yes, my son."

"I wonder if the days are not soon to be fulfilled in which the sorrows of our people will be ended. Listen to these words of Jeremiah." He unrolled a scroll and, laying his hands down flat on its surface, read: "In those days they shall say no more, the fathers have eaten sour grapes and the children's teeth are set on edge. But everyone shall die for his own iniquity: every man that eateth sour grapes, his teeth shall be set on edge."[2]

"But what says that word to us?" the mother asked.

"This: if we are not punished for the sins of our fathers, we will be rewarded for our own righteousness. Rome is not the penalty for the sin of any but ourselves. Had we a leader from among our people to stir us with a sense of our own moral obligations and promise us a destiny which our own deeds can win . . ." He was excited at the prospect, and as he lifted his hands to emphasize his words, the scroll furled itself with a shudder. He looked at it and laughed. "That's the way the mind of a Pharisee acts."

During the spring there were many times when his nimble mind picked up a word of wisdom from the ancient books, and lighted it with new understanding and promise, and ever the

[2] Jeremiah 31:29-30.

heart of his mother was glad, and the future brightened whenever she dared to anticipate it.

And then the portent of death invaded the little house
again. One evening the young man complained of a throbbing
agony underneath his heart, and all through the ominous
night his mother tended him, brewing homely medicines, and
cooling his burning forehead with wet napkins. But in the
morning, as the top of Tabor picked up the first signal of the
day and flashed it on to Carmel by the sea, the boy grew
limp and silent, and his breathing as gentle as the utter mo-
tionlessness of death. His mother stood up and walked bravely
to the door. The stillness of the dawn still pervaded the
village. She would not rouse the neighbors; it was too late for
help. She remembered the ancient story, endlessly told in
Nain, of the widow of Shunem, the village less than a mile
distant, and she wondered, for the moment, why in her day
no prophets were abroad, prophets who could lay themselves
upon a cold body and warm it back to life. When, she wondered, would Elijah come again?

She was surprised that so many shared her grief. She wished
for the boy's father that he too might share the sympathy that
they had denied him. And when, the next day, they carried
her beloved dead through the Horse Gate on the east side of
the village, she found herself thronged with mourners. Over
and over in her mind the words of Jeremiah repeated themselves: "A voice is heard in Ramah, lamentation and bitter
weeping, Rachel weeping for her children; she refuseth to be
comforted because they are not."[3] She said to herself that
she must not weep, that loyalty to the boy and his father
demanded strong, silent grief. But in spite of the reminiscence
and the resolution, she gave way to a convulsion of tears,
leaning momentarily against the bier to support herself.

"Weep not." She heard a strange voice, firm, commanding,
and infinitely tender. She looked through the mist of tears.

[3] Jeremiah 31:15.

A man was standing by the bier. He searched deftly among the grave clothes and put his hand firmly upon the young man's wrist. There was a convulsive shudder, and she heard the voice, firm, commanding and infinitely tender, say, "Young man, I say unto thee, Arise." The boy sat up, livid with the pallor of death, looked at his mother and smiled weakly, and then at the man who had touched him and said: ". . . dead bodies . . . ashes . . . all the fields . . . unto the Horse Gate toward the east . . . shall be holy unto Jehovah . . . nor thrown down forever."[4] When she reflected on it in later years she invariably remembered that she was neither terrified nor astonished at the restoration of the boy.

It was two years later when the young man set out for Jerusalem to attend the Passover. Since his strange resuscitation, life had seemed to him to challenge more and more of his energy and interest. The man, who was in a new sense the giver of life to him, had been back and forth through Galilee, and he had seen and heard him often. Here, he dimly thought, was the sort of man his father had hoped to be, the sort of teacher he himself had aspired to become. It was talked about the countryside that he was going to Jerusalem, and that his friends, of whom he had numbered multitudes, were going to make him king. And when, on the Sabbath before the festival, he found himself in a mob of pilgrims, shouting praises and escorting the Galilean into the city, his young heart leaped like a desert dancer. This was the fulfillment of the days, here was destiny revealed.

But five days later he was again outside the city in a noisy multitude of pilgrims. How mad, he thought, the change that had come over them. Today they were rejoicing in the death of the man they had acclaimed as king five days before. He was torn by anxiety and a desperate disappointment as he moved with the crowd upward toward the hill where three men

[4] Jeremiah 31:40.

hung on crosses. It was maddening—the blasphemy of those who dared to impugn the heroism of the central figure. He wanted to cry down their cruel and contemptuous words as the mob drifted near the crosses. And then, suddenly, as if face to face with doom, he found himself looking into the pain-pinched face of the man. He was aghast at the sight. The blood left his own face and he took on the leaden pallor of death as his eyes met the man's eyes in an agony of recognition. Here, he thought, was the loss of all the things he had cherished, the death of a dream he had loved, a vision he had pursued. The man must not die. The voices of the prophets and of his father cried within him and found utterance in his own words.

"If you are God's son," he cried, "come down from the cross. You must not die," he urged; "come down, come down." His voice was pleading, and his dark eyes, framed in his livid face, gave urgency to his words. He stood still amid the laughing, shouting crowd waiting some response from the face above him. There was a look of strong refusal. The young man reached up as if to touch him, but his hands clutched the tunic of his own garment at the throat, and rent it to the waist. The crowd swirled about him like a torrent of hate, and as he eddied away from the hill's dread summit he heard raucous voices taking up his plea derisively, and hurling it like shards of shattered fury in the sufferer's face: "come down—he is the king of Israel—ha, ha—let him now come down—we will believe him—he trusts in God—let him save him ——"

He pressed his hands over his ears and twisted blindly in the direction offering him quickest escape, but he did not have to run far before he found himself quite alone. He sat down, breathing heavily. The noise of the mob sounded dim and far away. He looked about him and discovered he was in a garden, a place of burial.

Part Two

THE CROSS AND LIBERALISM

Instead of the tireless competition for prizes for twenty-five-word essays on the superior qualities of Shinodent Tooth Paste, why not offer a reward for a fifty-word description of the first true liberal? History might be served, and autobiography enriched, and some obscure but worthy saint might even win his long conflict with oblivion and provide us, in his person, with a definitive norm for all subsequent discussions of liberalism. What such a contest might be worth would need an estimate by others than advertising agencies. It would perhaps deserve a prize too fabulous for even the manufacturers of dentifrice to hazard.

In default of such a hypothetical standard, one's discussion of so equivocal a term cannot escape bias. Liberalism cannot be as impotent as its traducers on the right say it is, nor can it be as out-of-date as its adversaries on the left insist. In fact it cannot be discussed in terms of potency, for of itself it has none; nor is an understanding of it to be won by fixing it in time, for, of itself, it is not dated. It can have only such powers as are contained in an abstract principle of criticism; it can have a life cycle only as extended as a standard of judgment. Therefore the first authentic liberal may have been the first homo that stood erect *because he wanted to*, because—that is to say—he discovered that it gave him an advantage over his fellows, conferred on him a measure of independence from the quadrupedal limitations he had accepted uncritically all his life. It may have made him a king, or it may have made him a snob, but in either case he deserves a monument.

Liberalism as a principle of criticism provides an estimate

of existence in terms of freedom, and freedom is only one of numerous words that indicates the quality of spirit it describes. Tolerance, complacency, independence, license, rebellion, exemption, emancipation—the list can be indefinitely extended. It may mean an aspiration; if so, he who aspires is a liberal, or it may be a condition. There is a philosophical understanding of the principle, a moral justification for it, and a social and individual experience of it. But above all, and of primary importance for our discussion, there is a religious ground for it.

One would hardly expect a religion that explained life in terms of Fate—Kharma of the Hindu or Kismet of the Muslim—to find much relevance in the concept of freedom. Historically this expectation is supported. It is therefore within the Hebrew-Christian tradition that the idea has flourished, though through a long period its growth was slow, stunted, and misunderstood. It took centuries to break out of the despot-slave conception of God and his creatures and to reach the father-son ideal. There is a story that a certain Egyptian king Akhnaton, who ruled a millennium-and-a-half B.C., distinguished himself with flashes of independent thought and rash courage. There must have been others like him who arose sporadically during countless thousands of years, some of whom were little more than freaks, others little less than philosophers. Otherwise the transition from savagery to civilization could not have occurred. But it was a long time before such independence of mind and action became something for which all men ideally might reach. This came about, within our own cultural tradition with the Hebrew prophets to whom our civilization stands in greater debt than we realize. Responsive to certain moral intuitions they exercised their protest against individual and social bondage, and invested the character of the God of Israel with the results of their thinking. Their influence was extraordinary in that it not only caused a change in outlook, but a qualitative change in life for the better, a change that moving up the heights of Isaiah and

Jeremiah and Amos, reached its apex in the life and teachings of Jesus. How far the promise of Jesus—"Ye shall know the truth and the truth shall make you free"—is from the experimental radicalism of King Akhnaton can be estimated only by an instrument delicate enough to register the growth of the soul of humanity.

Beyond a doubt the sense of freedom—one might almost as well call it independence or liberalism or individualism since the meanings are closely allied—dominated the early Christian movement. The followers of this new cult were conscious of a freedom from sin, religious legalism, and fear. They acted on this assumption in their defiance of Roman civil codes, in their provision for the physical well-being of the fellowship, and in their missionary adventures. Here was a new principle of fellowship, destined to be world wide. "If any man be in Christ Jesus he is a new creation," said Paul, meaning that he was not in bondage to the old laws of life. "Wherever the spirit of the Lord is, there is liberty." Little wonder that William Pitt said the Epistle to the Romans was the greatest treatise on liberty ever written.

Its fortunes fluctuated in terms of the historic context in which it found itself. Constantine imposed intolerable limits on the exercise of the liberal spirit. The Greek mind philosophized upon this simple life experience, and by reducing it to system made way for orthodoxy to hammer out a sword to use against the heretics, who have always been liberals, whether they were right or wrong. The rise and consolidation of the Holy Roman Empire finally reached the point of the dominance of all institutional life, both political and religious, and its suppression of the individual spirit was not to be effectively challenged until the rediscovery during the Renaissance of the inherent values in man. The florid days of that new intellectual springtime were warmed into life by a backward look toward the humanist poets of the Augustan age, the science of Aristotle and the moral dignity and simplicity of the early Christian movement. But the thrill of this reminiscence turned faces in other directions also, and in art, music, painting and literature, there was discovered in the immediate present the materials out of which free men might develop their lives.

If the Reformation and the rise of Democracy encouraged this individualistic liberalism, it was retarded again by Luther and Calvin who had none of the tolerance of Erasmus and Sir Thomas More. In the seventeenth century, Bacon, Newton, and John Locke provided the basis for a new rationalization of the essential greatness of the human spirit that was to be associated with the skeptical humanitarianism of the eighteenth century. The Quakers with the vital and moving experience of the Inner Light returned religious experience to the individual. Free and private apprehension of the divine was acknowledged and set in opposition to its mediation by priest or institution. The proliferation of Protestant sects was, in the religious world, the analogue of the ideas of private property, private amusement, private competition in business, and the right of private judgment.

The history of the calamities that visited liberal individualism in politics and economics is too familiar to need recounting here. Liberalism in politics became a compromise between the individualistic, competitive doctrine of strife and the optimistic doctrine of harmony. Competition between individuals was the way the universe proposed to bring about a stable civil society and a prosperous economic order. To believe in the brotherhood of man was no barrier to the most ruthless competition between men, and while this liberalism as a political force won—for a while—notable triumphs in Europe and America, a new industrial system was in the making that was to compromise and finally destroy the pretensions of economic liberalism. It needed only the criticism of the accepted doctrine of the soul by Hume, the Malthusian doctrine of the pressure of population on the means of subsistence, and the Mendelian doctrines of heredity, to complete the destruction of the intellectual grounds upon which the liberal doctrine of individualism had, we think falsely, rested.

For this reason it is customary today for radicals to heap obloquy on the liberal movement that sired laissez-faire capitalism, imperialism and war; and to regard with undisguised contempt the utilitarianism of Bentham and the Positivism of Auguste Comte, similarly spawned by the liberal mind. The rise of Marxism has spelled the defeat of the intellectual respectability of capitalism, and Freud has administered the *coup de grâce* to the naïve confidence of the human spirit in itself.

The result of this is a strange composite of anger, wistfulness and disillusionment. Men are angry that man has so misused the light within him, they are wistful for a return of confidence in themselves, and disillusioned by cheap and superficial shoddy that has been handed them by religious, political, and social theorists. Since Freud has cast suspicion on our rational processes, the only rational position that is defensible is a defense of irrationality. And since Marx sought to persuade the world that our economic destiny is the sport of irresistible material forces, we find the liberal man questioning whether, after all, his sense of freedom and urgency toward independent action is anything more than a monstrous mockery, staged by impersonal demonic forces to tease him ere he is destroyed.

But it is this very disquiet in the spirit of man that is the inextinguishable spark of liberalism. Were there no perturbation and disillusion, there would be no ground for trust in the liberal spirit. This is the strength of liberalism—and the word must not be dated, for it is timeless—that it forever stirs restlessly, that it can be critical of itself in terms of what it itself does for the human spirit, and that it will not allow any age or system or prophet to usurp or deny its right to think as wisely as it can, and act as righteously as it dares.

But the weakness of liberalism is close by its strength. The liberal distrust of cocksureness has tended to make for satisfaction with tentative and provisional positions. The debacle of liberal politics and economics has burnt liberal fingers. Since my display of confidence in an idea that I loudly expatiate upon may turn out, under psychoanalysis, to be an unconscious compensation for my fear that it is buncombe, therefore I must display confidence in nothing. I must not say loudly that I love my wife lest an astute observer detect in my ardor an unconscious wish to murder her. I must not be a zealot for democracy; it may be that I am overcompensating for a hidden phobia that has prevented my running for dogcatcher. And if I assert with a convincing show of emotional warmth my love for God and my fellowman, perhaps—not the Grand Perhaps of Browning, but a sniveling little psychiatric perhaps—I am getting ready to exploit the one or subvert the other. The modern liberal is likely not sure enough of anything to "go off the deep end" for it.

This has a consequence that is disturbing when it is seen to operate in the behavior of liberal religious leaders. To maintain an open mind involves a measure of tentativeness that gives a quality of freshness and resilience to one's mental processes. But since one cannot dissociate one's ideas about ideas from one's ideas about behavior, one runs the risk of being as morally equivocal as he is intellectually tentative. If moral codes of earlier days were insincere and socially and psychologically sterile or worse, then it is a great gain to expose them as such and be done with them. But it does not always follow that because Jonathan Edwards' concept of God is unacceptable to our generation, the moral code of that doughty saint is similarly so. There is a growing tendency among liberals—and for the moment we speak of religious liberals—to be as indulgent in personal habits as they are in personal opinions. There is a type of tolerance that can become as odious as it is weak. Nietzsche is reported to have said that Christianity ought to be purged of its moralic acid. Some liberals must have taken him seriously. One recalls what Ibsen had to say in *The League for Youth*:

Lundestad: I wasn't beaten; everything went just as I wanted. Stensgaard is not a man to make an enemy of; he has got what we others have to whistle for.

The Chamberlain: I don't quite understand what you mean ——?

Lundestad: He has the power of carrying people away with him. And then he has the luck to be unhampered by either character, or conviction, or social position; so that Liberalism is the easiest thing in the world for him.[1]

Liberalism that is easy or fortuitous is spurious or mere opportunism.

It is therefore an unhappy circumstance that finds many religious liberals so concerned to appear respectably liberal that they are indifferent to being thought respectably religious. Nor is it an accident that the emancipation from the stodgy orthodoxies, both of science and religion, that was won by many in the middle of the nineteenth century, was paralleled by a demand, on the part of a noisy few, for emancipation from the stuffy moralisms of the Victorian days. Only spiritual vigor and the practice of spiritual exercises will keep the liberal mood alive and warm. One notes with dismay the scorn of devotion and personal piety that much liberalism displays. Piety is the only safeguard against religious liberalism's decline to a desiccated and affected intellectualism or worse.[2] For the strength of liberalism is its sense of freedom.

[1] H. Ibsen, *The League for Youth:* Act 5, The Modern Library.

[2] "Edwards observed, with much truth, that 'these modern fashionable opinions, however called noble and liberal, are commonly attended, not only with a haughty contempt, but an inward malignant bitterness of heart, towards all the zealous professors of the contrary spiritual principles.'" N. B. Parker, *Jonathan Edwards, the Fiery Puritan,* Minton, Balch & Co., p. 237.

Professor Gilbert Murray says: (it) "is not a doctrine; it is a spirit or attitude of mind constantly changing in its outer manifestation according to the circumstances that it has to meet, but always essentially the same in itself, an effort *to get rid of prejudice* so as to see the truth, *to get rid of selfish passions* so as to do the right."[3]

It would seem that a great many liberals have never heard or have forgotten the admonition of one of the greatest in the liberal tradition. "For freedom did Christ set us free. Stand fast, therefore, and be not entangled in a yoke of bondage" (Galatians 5:1). It is easy for the pretensions of liberalism to become a yoke; it is easier, perhaps, for the behavior of liberals to become libertine—an old form of bondage. For when a man *must* say and do things in order to maintain his status as a liberal before himself as well as before others, he has already lost his freedom. His liberalism is sick, and conscious of its weakness, it boasts its health. To meet an arrogant liberal provides as unpleasant an encounter as meeting his unyielding opposite. One is no less repelled by a snob than by a bigot.

Jesus was a liberal. This is no partisan claim, for the standard that liberalism has set up derives from him. Not originally, or solely. The first liberal, we have said, is lost to history, but his successors have left their records. Every man who has sought, to use Professor Murray's words, "to get rid of prejudice so as to see the truth, to get rid of selfish passions so as to do the right" has been in the great succession, and they all have won a place in history because the prejudice and selfish passions of others marked them in every age for their own. But they were, nevertheless, the discoverers "of fresh insight, the recipients of new illumination, gifted leaders of

[3] *Liberality and Civilization,* The Hibbert Lectures, The Macmillan Company, p. 37.

unwon causes, prophets of neglected or forgotten truth, profound interpreters of the deeper significance of life."[4]

There is no need here to adduce evidence that Jesus was a part of this tradition. It has been done many times. We shall present subsequently the relation of the Cross principle to his liberalism as a unique and profound contribution to the liberal spirit. But it is interesting to note that at his trial, his liberalism and all it involved of political and religious irregularity when called to account, revealed itself as plausible, forthright and adamant. Confronted by questions as to his teaching—this was, in effect, a challenge to his liberalism—he deferred generously to those who had heard him speaking in the Temple (John 18:20), and agreed to stand by such testimony as they gave. This was so different from the reply expected from a rabbi—whose defense was supposed to be in the inviolable law—that an officer interpreted it as insolence, and struck him. In Jesus' reply to his assailant we have an epitome of the liberal mind: he asked for a refutation of his statement instead of leaping to a dogmatic defense of himself —"and if I have said anything wrong, prove it" (Moffatt)— and he acknowledged thereby the possibility of his being wrong and his willingness to argue the point; and at the same time he conceded the right of his adversary to protest, but only *after he had been proved in error*. This demonstration is rarely suggested as a cause of the high-priestly consternation that followed, but one wonders whether anything else that was said or done during his trial, could have had a more disconcerting effect on those who sat in judgment on him. It stands to this good hour as a pattern for all those whose aggressive pursuit of goodness and truth has brought them in conflict with the modern high priests of orthodox thought and conduct.

Jesus' discovery—and it must have been, as it must always

[4] Rufus Jones, *The Church's Debt to Heretics*, Doubleday Doran Co., page 12.

be, a personal one—that it is a knowledge of the truth that sets one free, is the most frequently quoted of his insights into life. And properly so, for within those words are contained a complete philosophy of life: "Ye shall know"—the function of life; "the truth"—the fact of life; "and the truth shall make you free"—the fulfillment of life. But in his own working out of that philosophy he bequeathed to liberalism its most priceless heritage, the moral dynamic by which liberalism is to be saved from "falling under a yoke of bondage." It was the Cross. But before we seek to face up to it, it may help us to go back to the episode with which this chapter was introduced.

The tendency of all liberalism, we have said, is toward tolerance of opinions and judgments differing from one's own. Since all of life is tentative and every presupposition by which we live is relative, there is always the possibility that the faith of today may be the folly of tomorrow. Huxley said, "All ideas begin as heresies and end as superstitions," and while he was certainly sacrificing scientific accuracy to sententiousness, he was expressing something of the liberal feeling of the constant need for re-examination of our credos and an adaptation of our ideas to our experiences. It is this that brings both the excitement of novelty and the danger of inaction to the liberal mind. In the episode, the young man of Nain, chastened in his own enthusiasm by recollections of the misfortunes his father's radicalism had brought on his mother and himself, sought to indulge the delights of liberalism without accepting its obligations. And fearing the young preacher in whom he had found such spiritual refreshment was likely to lose everything by going to the limits his quest for truth and freedom demanded of him, he pled with him to come down from the cross. The cross is no place for a liberal; it ill befits his tolerance and his urbanity! For the criminal who undervalues the law and for the fanatic who overvalues it, the cross is a proper and perhaps inescapable consequence. But even in a world of relative values, death by its nature is definitive, and by its results irremediable, and therefore is left outside the pattern of voluntary liberal behavior. And this has proved true, dramatically and terrifyingly true, in the past ten years. The liberal mind, overcome by moral lethargy, has been disorganized and stampeded by the fanatics or criminals—no matter how one may choose to put it—of a new and ruthless dogmatism. There is no lack of willingness on their part to go off the deep end for what they say is right, and for what they propose to win.

It is just here that the Cross furnishes us the supreme example of intellectual vigor linked with moral strength. There are those who object to reducing the Cross to the status of an example. There is certainly no justification for reducing the Cross for any purpose, but there is no derogation of its meaning in finding in it the compulsion that all exemplary heroism exerts. And if the Cross is—as we strongly believe—the dramatization of the principle that alone makes the universe orderly and its ends worthy of deity—then there are aspects of its operation in every area where action occurs. We may pass over the question whether Jesus could have come down from the cross and saved himself. As always, one's answer to that depends on one's presuppositions. But the fact is that he did not come down, either because of impotence, disinclination or high purpose, and his dying for his faith still stands above the low levels of man's ethical achievements like a peak marking the ultimate altitude of humanity's moral accomplishment. Nor is the Cross of Christ disparaged by being placed, at this point of our discussion, in the category of the hemlock of Socrates, or the pyre of Ridley and Latimer. Every act of uttermost devotion to a cause has its moral nobility and inspiration, and as such participates in the quality that makes the Cross redemptive.

The strength of liberalism, we repeat, is in its sense of freedom. It follows therefore that its altars must always be

kept aglow with the fires that are the evidence of faithful
votaries who tend them. This is as true in politics, economics,
and world affairs as in religion. The decline of the liberal
spirit always marks the decline of faith, hope and love. If
there is ash instead of flame at the heart of the faiths of
modern paganism, it is because they have never known or
have lost the ineffable vision of freedom, or have nurtured
a spirit

> . . . fevered by an inner fire,
> That finds no fuel underneath a spire,
> And dying, sweeps its ashes and its spark
> Into the cruel silence of the dark.

A liberalism kept fresh and powerful by its sense of freedom
will pass judgment on life in terms of the measure of freedom
it has won and shared, and will indict as wicked all things
that fetter and enslave even the least of one of God's little
ones. Therefore Christian liberalism must keep alive by
keeping free, and if the Son shall make it free, it shall be
liberal indeed. This seems to us to mean that the moment
liberalism lends an attentive ear to the proposal that it come
down from the Cross and save itself, it shall have entered
already into a conspiracy with a despot that will enslave it
utterly.

The verdict the immediate present will pass on this type
of liberalism will perhaps not be a wholly sympathetic one.
The plea to come down from the Cross will come not from
one's enemies but from one's friends, from those who share
one's faith, but who lack the courage to die for it. And the
crowds will go away, and leave the victim, desolate and alone,
upon the hill. At the same time it is a quality of the liberal
faith that it trusts in the long-term verdict, in the final victory and vindication of truth and freedom, and it shall therefore abide the anger of enemy and the disappointment of
friend until the final judgment is handed down.

This was, of course, the experience of him who refused to come down from the Cross, and gave to the liberal mind its perfect exemplar. But with him the verdict was not so long deferred as his friends would have expected had they had the wit and composure to think in terms of judgment. The mob that came to scoff, returned at once beating their breasts in what was surely the prelude to Pentecost, and seventy years after Calvary an old man said: "We have seen his glory—glory such as an only son enjoys from his father—seen it to be full of grace and reality" (John 1:14, Moffatt). To be full of reality does not mean to be filled up with correct ideas. That would come nearer being an orthodox than a liberal understanding. It means rather to be utterly faithful, with the fidelity of the tide to the moon, or the magnetic needle to the pole. And grace? This is a description of one's manner—full of graciousness. What a picture! Here was one whose utter fidelity to truth found a freedom so perfect that he was seen moving unhampered, free, gracefully, with a glory such as an only son enjoys from his father!

"Of his fulness we all received, and grace for grace (his grace added to our grace?). For the law was given through Moses; grace and truth came through Jesus Christ" (John 1:16-17. A.R.).

CHAPTER SIX

Part One

NICODEMUS AND JOSEPH

"Do you remember the answer I got when I asked why he was being judged without a trial?" Nicodemus was talking with his elder friend Joseph of Ramathaim-Gilead. They were seated in the lecture hall of Nicodemus' home. All of the pupils had gone, for it was the time of the midday recess and Joseph, patron of the rabbi's school, had lingered for further conversation.

"No," answered Joseph, "I do not recall."

"Well, it was the same old evasion," continued Nicodemus. "No effort was made to answer my question. Instead, they began abusing me. They had cursed the mob because of its ignorance of the law. Perhaps they would have cursed me also, save that my knowledge of the law is greater than theirs. So they simply called me a Galilean, I who have never lived anywhere but here." His long white hands gestured to indicate the place where they were seated. "And then they said that if I knew anything at all, I surely knew that no prophet could come out of Galilee."

"A not too indirect way of saying that your word was of no worth," put in Joseph. "First they asked you if you were not from the province of Galilee, and then observed that those who were could claim not the rank of prophet."

"Nay, I am no prophet," corrected Nicodemus modestly, "nor am I a Galilean. But their abuse of me was no answer to my question."

Joseph was an imposing figure as he sat on a stone bench by the wall. The bright light of the sixth hour, dimmed by a heavy cloud, suffused the long room through narrow grated windows with an early premonition of nightfall, and the severe elegance of his appearance and bearing seemed to grow rather than diminish in the gray light. Born to great wealth in Gilead and learned in the wisdom of the Greeks, he was, nevertheless, a devout and careful seeker after God. He had outlived the contempt for the lore of his own people that in his youthful years he had boasted. The wealth of his family that attracted greedy Roman officials and employed Greek tutors, had only momentarily satisfied the longings of his eager spirit, and it was not many years until the avarice of the one and the dilettantism of the other turned him in disappointment back to the messianic hopes of the great prophets of his own race. Out of Rome would come no suffering servant so long as the sword was the symbol of power, and out of Greece would come no redemption so long as the bower of Epicurus was a shrine and the rational discipline of Zeno and Cleanthes was the ritual of piety. And yet he had found the Pharisees dull, unimaginative and disputatious, more concerned with argument than with seeking; they were divided into competing and quarrelsome sects, obscuring the truth by which the spirit of man lives under the rubbish of controversy by which the soul of man dies. He was, indeed, arrived at the point where soured by disillusion he was ready to abandon the society of men to become a desert hermit. Then he met young Nicodemus.

Here was a man whose wisdom was prodigious and whose spirit was gentle. Born to moderate wealth he was, nevertheless, raised in a cultural tradition that set great store by austerity of life and thought. Generous without ostentation, his right hand knew not what his left hand gave away; pious without display, he uttered his prayers in secret to a God who, seeing in secret, had rewarded him openly. In such a man, though he was younger than himself by a score of years, Joseph found a true fellow of the spirit.

"That was six moons ago," went on Nicodemus, "and I find

them less reasonable now than then. Yesterday they seemed consumed with a desire to destroy him."

"Why is it, Rabbi, that it is the teachers of religion who destroy the seekers after truth? Not the teachers of philosophy, who are often tolerant to the point of being ambiguous?"

"Perhaps," answered Nicodemus slowly, "perhaps it is because religion becomes so easily the vested interest of a class." He paused and added soberly, "Of my class."

"But you would not destroy him."

"No; he may be God's anointed. Who can tell? Many who have spoken God's truth have died for it, and it is always at the instigation of those who have a stake in the preservation of the established order." He was speaking with mounting enthusiasm as was his habit before his pupils, and the agitation of his hands kept pace with the rising modulations of his resonant voice. He paused momentarily as a servant, entering the room, bowed low and waited until his master had ceased speaking to ask whether they were ready to eat. Nicodemus dismissed him, with an almost impatient gesture.

"What is it that the Sanhedrin seeks to do to this Galilean? What evil has he done except to speak the truth about those of us who teach the law, and to cry a bane on the head of the high priest. We cannot endure it, nor can Annas, and . . ."

"And is he not a rabbi?"

"Aye, by the consent of those who hear him gladly, but not by the consent of the schools. Even thus does he turn the hearts of the people away from us, and for this reason they say he must die."

"Why 'they' and not 'we'?" It was a way Joseph had of bringing issues to a personal focus. His companion was quick to see his point and answer it.

"I would not have him silenced, much less condemned. I speak to you as Nicodemus. But I, like yourself, am also a member of the Sanhedrin, and there we must speak a cautious, corporate word. To defend him there or to follow him openly among the people, well . . ."

Nicodemus stood up. The disturbance in his spirit was marked by the restlessness of his body. He walked back and forth before Joseph, combing his full beard with long nervous fingers. "And yet," he resumed finally, "there is no little peril in what he teaches, not only to us who know, but to the simpler folk who have followed him hither. 'Except a grain of wheat fall into the ground and die,' it was thus he spoke yesterday in the temple. Such is the law of wheat. But is no man more than wheat? Has not Israel died under the heel of oppression, and borne no fruit but a generation of servile and suppliant slaves? 'Born of the spirit,' he says; yet was not Elijah so born, and is not every one, indeed, breathed on from the nostrils of Jehovah. I think . . ." Here he turned suddenly and faced his companion, his eyes burning with the fire of his ardent soul, "I think that I would follow him, but for his talk of death."

Joseph, who had stayed seated, engrossed in the conflict that agitated his young teacher's mind, finally stood up. "Shall we not eat a morsel to refresh us?" He was more concerned to quiet his friend than to propose a meal, and as he walked toward the door he clapped his hands smartly. A servant appeared at once and Joseph despatched him to call his own menial who was waiting orders in an outer court. When he appeared, his master sent him out into the street with an order to fetch a savory meat and a flagon of sweet wine from a favorite shop. When he turned back into the room, Joseph asked: "What did the Sanhedrin do with him this morning?"

"I do not know; I stayed away. Did you not go?"

"No," answered Joseph in amazement. "The hour was early, and I had given orders that I was not to be disturbed. Besides I have no taste for that crowd when they are quarreling. But I was sure you would be there." Nicodemus moved toward the door in long strides and called loudly to his servant who appeared at once, like an echo to his summons. "Have you heard any talk among the common folk of a Galilean teacher in the city?" he asked agitatedly.

"Aye, sir," the young man answered. "About the middle of the fourth hour I heard the noise of rioting in the great street before the praetorium. I asked a water carrier, who came along later, what had happened, and he said three men had been taken out to die. One, he said, was a teacher from Galilee."

The servant bowed and withdrew, and almost immediately the personal menial of Joseph appeared in the door, balancing a tray. Nicodemus stepped aside and he entered, advanced to the table and set his burden down. Joseph, who in astonishment, and with not a little trepidation had heard the answer of Nicodemus' servant, asked his own man: "Did you hear word of the Galilean teacher?"

"Aye," he answered carelessly; "a lad at the shop said he had just come from an execution. A Galilean was already dead when he left; two thieves are still alive."

"The Galilean is dead, so soon?" he asked incredulously.

"Aye, and when he cried out, a black cloud covered the sky. Men were afraid and scattered like sheep."

Nicodemus did not speak. He stood for a moment biting his lip, and then slumped heavily onto a couch. The servant went about preparing the meal for the two men, but when he announced it ready, both disdained to eat.

Joseph of Ramathaim-Gilead lost no time after learning of the death of Jesus. Accompanied by his servant, he made his way through the city to the palace of the governor. He was not unknown to the palace guard, but he was subjected to a somewhat scrupulous examination before he was allowed to enter. When at length he was ushered into the governor's presence, he made short shrift of the conventional nothings that ordinarily introduced a request for a favor. Instead he went to the point of his request almost brusquely.

"I have come to ask the body of Jesus of Nazareth," he said sharply, "and I bring a modest gift to honor your excellency." He knew that the corpses of criminals were cast into the loathsome pit of Gehenna, the public dump, and unless claimed by friends or kinsfolk would feed the packs of savage dogs that ranged like wolves, outside the city walls. He knew also Pilate's reputation; he would sell a permit for anything, but sell it dearly, and Joseph was prepared to buy the privilege of disposal, however costly it proved. Furthermore, Joseph was known for his wealth, and the governor, never lenient with poor suppliants, was always hard on rich ones.

"The body of Jesus of Nazareth," Pilate answered with a bitter smile. "Would I could give you the twin spots his eyes burned into my soul, the bruise that one word of his left on my heart. It will not soon heal."

"One cannot pay adequately enough to assure healing to heart and soul," answered Joseph, "but your price for the body cannot be too dear."

"Dear," echoed Pilate. "Take your friend, if such he be, and say nothing about price. My wife warned me that he would cost me more than gold can redeem. I washed my hands of him, but he will not wash away. You would buy him out of my hands, but your gold cannot remove him. Take him, and begone, and bury him deep and remote lest he return to plague my sleep with new visions."

He turned to a man at his elbow and gave him an order for the release of the body. He gave the name as Joseph, and hurriedly pressed his seal in the warm wax the secretary made ready. As he handed the permit to Joseph he eyed him narrowly and said slowly: "Joseph of Ramathaim-Gilead; are you Joseph of the family of Arimathea, weaver of fine woolens, maker of choice wines?" It was dawning on his harassed mind that he was releasing for nothing a privilege that could have been dearly sold. He had not, for the moment, identified his visitor. Most of the followers of the Galilean were simple, poor folk. He reached out his pudgy hand and took the permit from Joseph and read it again. His palms itched for the bribe he had so carelessly lost.

"Will you accept . . . ?" Joseph interrupted his hesitation.

"No, what I have written, I have written," the governor replied pompously.

In the meantime, Nicodemus overcome with a strange and dispiriting weariness had gone to his bedchamber. "Dead," he said repeatedly. "I might have said a word to warn him. Perhaps he dared too recklessly the wrath of the Sanhedrin. He disparaged the faith of the simple and challenged the wisdom of the wise. Can one mend the behavior of men except he make more rigid the demand of our laws? To promise freedom to all who know the truth is to doom to unimportance those who teach the law."

And then his mood changed again. He was overwhelmed with the compassion of the man and his scorn of fear. Dead he might be, but what happened to such as he after the body was dead. Nicodemus had argued with the Sadducees who denied the resurrection, but would they—could they—base their denials on such vital spirits as this man who had just died? "Except a grain of wheat die." The words returned to his uncomfortable mind. He got up from his couch and stood by a window. The cloud that had so strangely blacked out the world an hour ago was gone; but the sun seemed unable to disperse the pallor that despite the cloudless sky, still pervaded the lifeless air. "Except it die," the words recurred. And then he almost startled himself by saying with a vehemence he could not account for: "Die? Well, he is dead! Now let him bring forth much fruit!"

He heard a sound in the courtyard beneath the window. It was Joseph and his servant. After leaving the palace, they had hurried to the narrow alley where the sellers of perfumes and spices protected their perishable wares against the full sunlight in dingy little shops. Joseph was prodigal in his spending. The shopkeepers were amazed that he would not haggle for prices, and the amount of unguents, pungent aloes, and fragrant spices he bought was sufficient for the burial of a king. As Nicodemus descended the stairway he met his friend in the narrow hall. "We shall have his body, I have the permit from the governor. He who had not our protection in life shall have it in death."

"But," remonstrated Nicodemus, "what of his disciples?"

"They have asked for nothing from Pilate, and it is reported in the city that they are fled for fear that they shall share the fate of their friend."

"And the Sanhedrin? They are not fled; and did they know that we who are of their number honor their adversary in death?"

"Have you a winding sheet? Fine linen it shall be; and napkins?" Joseph seemed not to have heard the last question, and it was well. Nicodemus turned and disappeared. The recklessness of his trusted friend was, for the moment, the answer to his own fears. He went to a large wooden chest in his bedchamber, opened it and took out a bolt of linen, soft as satin, which had never been used. Years before, as her gift to his burial, his mother had prepared it and put it away, and it released the delicate old fragrance of essence of myrrh as he unwound it layer by layer. At the center he found crushed dry petals of asphodel blossoms, the flower of death. "Except it die," he said again, as the brown fragments drifted to the floor. The man of Galilee would sleep forever in the linens of Nicodemus.

It was already well on toward sunset, and Joseph was eager to reach the place of death before the bodies were removed. He and a servant and Nicodemus were seen by few as they left the house by a back door and, avoiding the busier streets, made their way around to the gate of Herod, and thence to Skull Hill. They approached the hill from the west and came first to Joseph's garden. There, amid a profusion of spring flowers, was the newly hewn grotto he had prepared for his own burial. They went cautiously inside, and deposited their freight of linen and spices on a stone shelf, and leaving the servant on guard, went on up the hill to its bare summit.

The crowds that a little more than an hour before had surged like a tide over the place were almost gone. The two thieves were hanging limp and lifeless. Bloody lacerations on body and legs indicated their death had been hastened by the executioners. Over to one side, they saw a guard of soldiers idling about. Near them three women were bending over the body of the Galilean. His mother was holding his head in her lap, weeping softly as she bent above his face.

Joseph showed his permit to the guard. To them it was a simple routine but the centurion in charge manifested a strange interest in the request. There was something almost gentle and even reverent in the way he approached the women. It was through his kindness that the body of Jesus had been removed from the cross, and so when he approached them again, they graciously admitted his interruption. For a moment they were dismayed at what they thought was the loss of the body, but they were quickly reassured that the two strangers had come to offer burial in a garden close by.

Nicodemus and Joseph, aided by two of the soldiers, lifted the limp form gently, and followed by the three still bewildered and incredulous women, disappeared below the crest of the hill. And there, for an hour, in the cool moist interior of the new grotto, gentle hands anointed the body with aromatics of fabulous worth and enfolded it in a linen cerement of the most delicate texture and fragrance.

Three soldiers rolled a heavy stone across the opening of the newly tenanted sepulcher. Three men, turning toward the city in the twilight, looked back across the top of the hill and saw three crosses against the somber and gathering darkness; and three women sat in a garden, their hands still redolent of myrrh and their hearts still numb with sorrow and wonder.

secrecy with which they maintained their orthodoxy. Their magic, their healing arts, and their amazing knowledge of astronomy and natural law were all occult and private, and because the common man could not know, and therefore could not tinker with orthodoxy, the power of priest was at all times only slightly less than that of the pharaohs, and sometimes even usurped royal prerogatives.

The exodus of the children of Israel under the leadership of Moses was a liberal revolution inspired by the faith of a great and daring pioneer. Had Moses been less of a rebel, the longing for the fleshpots would have turned the people back into slavery; had he been less than a liberal, he would not have been the medium of the enormously significant experiences at the base and on the summit of Sinai where the code of Hammurabi was sharpened and elevated by the lifting vision of an awe-ful and powerful Jehovah, to become the moral base upon which the structure of human living for half the world was to be erected. As time went on and the vicissitudes of struggle and accomplishment modified the shape and texture of life, the orthodoxy of that great people was solidified, and its values were safeguarded by penalty and public opinion. When, however, orthodoxy became the enemy of godliness—as it often did, and does, for in a strange way theology sometimes becomes the enemy of ethics—great men of God challenged formalism in the interests of vitality, and while they nearly always got in trouble for their pains, they quite as often saved their generations from spiritual death. From Egypt to Judea orthodoxy provided solidarity; from Moses to the Maccabees, liberalism provided progress.

It is a commonplace that Jesus encountered an orthodoxy in his day that was not to be done away, lest religious and moral cohesion disintegrate, but was to be fulfilled in order that religion and morals should not die. He got into trouble, to be sure. Whenever one says: "This is the way it has always been done, but . . ." he invites trouble. That little adversative conjunction is the pivot upon which revolution always turns. He did not deride the wisdom or disparage the righteousness of the orthodox; he only demanded that their wisdom fructify and that their righteousness bring forth fruit. They were neither stupid nor evil, they were wise and good, and that was their peril; for wisdom and rectitude for them were stereotyped and statistical, and even while they preserved the letter of the law and counted their tithes, slavishly and jealously, the blight of moral and spiritual death was upon them. His sin, in their eyes, was his challenge to orthodoxy; their sin, in his view was their subservience to it. He, they charged, had threatened to destroy the temple. It has always been a part of the faith of orthodoxy that spiritual vandalism—as all liberalism is thought to be—must be dealt with in a summary fashion, and this they proceeded to do. The irony of the situation was that their repudiation of Jesus created a new and invincible wisdom and righteousness which overwhelmed them. It is also ironic that even to this good hour, an emulation of the spirit of Jesus almost invariably invites an emulation of his fortunes.

This is by no means to say that the substitution of anarchy for orthodoxy is the means of salvation. The significance of thought is to be found in the capacity of the mind to come to conclusions. Only as man adds conclusion to conclusion, doctrine to doctrine, yes, and dogma to dogma, can he bring direction to aimlessness in thought, and only thus does he fulfill the function for which his mind is given him. To refuse to submit to a system of ideas, or to boast that one is through with all finalities, or has outgrown all definitions, is to sink gradually back into the vagueness of dreams or the impulsiveness of subhuman behavior. For mental advance there must be the construction of a definite philosophy of life, a philosophy which one must believe is as right as others are wrong. But within that philosophy there must be more than dogmatics, there must be dynamics; it must include as a rudiment the dogma that while A is so right today that one will die for it, A may be so wrong tomorrow, that one will be done with it. All the while the mind must be kept sufficiently supple so that a demonstration that A is wrong will not result in the collapse of the system of ideas that has included it. This is what has taken place over and over again in the fields of science, economics, politics and philosophy. The rejection of an idea that has been proved to be wrong, even though for generations it was undisputed, has always been regarded as a victory for science. The theory of abiogenesis was accepted from Aristotle's day until 1870, but its definitive rejection by Pasteur, after proof of its error, was one of the greatest of all scientific accomplishments, albeit the Academy of the Normal School in Paris penalized Pasteur by refusing him membership for his presumptuous heresy. The base on which science rested was not weakened by that surrender, it was strengthened. Illustrations of the displacement of old error by the discovery of new truth and a consequent strengthening of the bases of knowledge in economics, politics and general philosophy are too abundant to need specification. It is the most persistent and mischievous of errors that removes religion from the operation of this general law. Paul was under no illusions here. "As a wise master builder I have laid a foundation; and *another buildeth* thereon" (I Corinthians 3:10) . The fear of building with all it involves has rested like a blight over Christendom since the fifth century; but Paul saw more need for structuralists than for fundamentalists in the Christian economy. If a similar bit of fundamental wisdom by Hippocrates had been treated with the indifference Paul's exhortation has received, we would still be exorcising demons instead of practicing medicine, and our treatment of mental illness would be black magic instead of psychiatry.

Orthodoxy, no matter where it is, can be obstinate and vindictive, and generally is. Nowhere more than in government is stereotype guarded more vigilantly, and in times of emergency its protectors are as blind as the priests of religion.

Whether a statement is true is unimportant so long as a majority opinion accepts its opposite. The most egregious violations of democratic principles may be called democratic, and protest against such abuses called subversive.[1] And when rival orthodoxies pit their strength against each other and call on their partisan gods to bless them, the spectacle is depressing beyond words to describe. What can be more discrediting to free people than the fury of the prophets of democracy against Jehovah's witnesses in this year of grace 1940, or what more dispiriting than the zealous and infallible pretensions of the witnesses as they are uttered against all governments and all sects. Here is orthodoxy that yields nothing, learns nothing, and wins nothing.

It is this feeling of infallibility, in some cases carefully formulated and boldly proclaimed, and in others deeply felt but not explicitly confessed, that is the bane of orthodoxy. It may be the result of sheer spiritual arrogance; it may be a disguise that fear of the truth wears. The former rationalizes itself in terms of a divine commission; the latter in terms of a revelation once for all delivered. But arrogance and fear are toxic and their poisons inevitably sicken the spirit and lay waste the most important of all our secondary spiritual powers, humility, secondary only because it is customarily regarded as a passive virtue. Inability or disinclination to confess to limitation or failure is a symptom of spiritual paralysis of the gravest sort, spiritual paralysis in spite of the fact that it is generally true that orthodoxy makes much of the spiritual evidences or façades of its faith. If liberalism is vexed by the tentativeness of its faith, orthodoxy is plagued by its infallibility; if liberalism drifts in the direction of cold intellectualism, orthodoxy may miss falling into the fire of undisciplined emo-

---

[1] The passage of the Conscription Act is a perfect illustration of the way it is possible to take something which in itself is inherently *un*democratic and by *calling* it democratic disarm the suspicions of those on whom it is imposed.

tionalism by the narrowest of margins; if the liberal will not die for anything, the orthodox may, if not very careful, die for nothing.

Infallibility, however, is a fiction difficult to maintain. The sense of indefectibility is as rare in sane persons as its non-existence in insincere ones. Pretentions to infallibility are pathological; no man who has shut the door to meet his heavenly Father in secret would dare to greet him with a claim to parity on the level of omniscience. "Normally speaking, the greater a man is, the less likely he is to make the very greatest claim. . . . Nobody can imagine Shakespeare talking as if he were literally divine; though we might imagine some crazy American crank finding a cryptogram in Shakespeare's works, or preferably in his own works."[2] For this reason orthodoxy relies on something external to itself to buttress its claims. It creates an institution. As is the case with corporations, which have no soul, institutions are similarly unembarrassed. It is the soul of man that rebukes his impulse to boast of spiritual certitude; a soulless institution knows no such restraints. It is *ex cathedra*, not *ex cordis*, utterances that are never wrong, and it is out of the abundance of the heart that the mouth speaketh (*Ex abundantia enim cordis os loquitur*).

Such an institution may be no more than a formulation of ideas into a creed. The first great councils of the Christian church felt this need and met it; and while there were individuals, no doubt, to whom some of the phrases were obscure, not to say preposterous, the moment they were accepted, they were vested with inviolable authority. Such was the inspiration in the mind of Constantine when he called the first Ecclesiastical Council to meet at Nicaea in Bithynia in 325, and it was the original Nicene Creed that hurled the first anathemas at the heretics, seeking thus to terrify them into conformity. It is interesting to note that subsequent creeds, after the institu-

[2] Gilbert K. Chesterton, *The Everlasting Man,* Dodd, Mead & Co., p. 247.

tional tendency became explicit in an hierarchy, deleted the threats to the faithless. Naturally so; such became the prerogative of the head of the Church. Naturally also the status of a vested interest was claimed by and conferred upon the institution. And so began the age-long tendency which culminated in 1870 in the proclamation of the doctrine of Papal Infallibility. The issue of this sort of thing is beyond the scope of our study, but it is instructive to observe that the self-styled orthodox branch of the Catholic Church, from which all others have withdrawn, went to the uttermost extremes of pretentiousness, and was finally liquidated as an enemy of the people. Is this to be the end of all man's claims to infallibility?

But not all of the claims of institutional support for infallibility are within the Roman and Greek traditions. Whenever a creed goes beyond statement to claim, whenever it is regarded, not as a formula, but as a policeman, it has fallen into the institutional pattern. Woe betide the man then who disputes it. And this is as true of the creeds of economics and politics as of religion. The man who defies a creed is a heretic; the man who defers to a creed is an institutionalist.

There is another resource available to the man who must maintain the fiction of infallibility. It is not an institutional or corporate aid; it is what he calls Conscience. This instrument is not the Censor of Freudianism, nor the wisdom that cometh down from above that is "first pure, then peaceable, gentle, easy to be entreated, full of mercy and good fruits, without variance, without hypocrisy" (James 3:17). It is a sergeant-at-arms that steps in arbitrarily and stops dispute, after which no consideration either of truth or propriety will allow continuance of debate. The moment one says: "my conscience tells me," the order of the day is suspended. And therein rests an interesting paradox: the claim of the liberal to exercise his independence of thought may lead him to the liveliest, and even the most absurd speculations; but the orthodox exercising his independence of conscience generally comes to rest in a safe and respectable conformity to conventionalism.

We have been saying that orthodoxy represents an invaluable quality of the human spirit—the impulse to convert facts into truth and truth into dogma. Similarly liberalism is to be jealously protected and deepened. Chesterton in *Heretics* exhorted: "Let us, then go upon a long journey and enter on a dreadful search. Let us, at least, dig and seek till we have discovered our own opinions. . . . The skepticism of our time does not really destroy the beliefs, rather it creates them; gives them their limits and their plain and defiant faith."[3] Such was his faith as a liberal in 1909. Later he was to write: "In the Catholic Church, there are still those headlong acts of holiness that speak of something rapid and recent; a self-sacrifice that startles the world like a suicide. . . . It is newer in spirit than the newest schools of thought; and it is most certainly on the eve of new triumphs."[4] That was his faith as a Catholic in 1925. It would seem that he was able to combine in his spirit both the urgency and flow of liberalism and the solid certitude of orthodoxy. It is when orthodoxy becomes infallible that it loses its vitality; and it is only when liberalism is willing to lose its life that it becomes infallible. If some regard Protestantism as the "nadir of nothingness" as a writer some years ago put it, and point out that the right of independent judgment ends in atomism or anarchy, the Protestant spirit—at its best in the liberal mind—must prove itself *morally* competent to deal with anarchy. If Catholicism is regarded as an escape from the discipline of personal research, it must show itself *intellectually* competent to survive without pretensions to infallibility.

It is at this point that the Cross principle becomes relevant

[3] Gilbert K. Chesterton, *Heretics*, John Lane Company, 1909, pp. 303-304.
[4] Gilbert K. Chesterton, *The Everlasting Man*, Dodd, Mead & Co., p. 338.

to our discussion. As we spoke of liberalism, the point was made that the Cross was a dramatization of that willingness to die for an idea, even though it be—as it was in Jesus' case—regarded as heresy. It is unwillingness to die for an idea that is the most conspicuous weakness of liberalism. To come down from the cross was the sensible thing to do from the liberal viewpoint. A great deal more was to be won for the cause of the Kingdom of God by stopping short of extreme measures, than by dying for it. After all, his public ministry had only extended over three short years. Would it not have been better to conciliate the moment in the hope of conquering the generation? So spoke the voice of liberalism on the lips of the young man of Nain. And not until liberalism is willing to die for its faith will its faith be validated. The moral example of the Cross still confronts the sometimes equivocal and sometimes cowardly liberalism of today.

As the Cross principle impinges on the orthodox mind the situation is somewhat different. The orthodox willingness to die for its ideas has often vitiated its faith. So as the Cross confronts the tendency toward the infallibility, dogmatics and authoritarianism that is implicit in orthodoxy, the demand it makes is in line with orthodoxy's deepest need. Recall again the simile with which Jesus pictured the principle. "Except a grain of wheat fall into the ground and is diffused, it abides alone; but if it is diffused, it fructifies." Recall also the insistence that this principle must apply to all life or to none of it. It remains to ask how such a simile can represent action in the region of dogmatics.

It is a commonplace of speech that refers to ideas as being living. There is nothing, someone has wisely observed, so irresistible as an idea whose time has come. This may be thought to refer to the energy that expels an idea from its matrix, an energy that must bring to birth or destroy; or it may be regarded as an army on the march against which no defense is effective. We prefer the former figure, for it brings again to mind the grain of wheat. How prodigious indeed is the power of a seed that, having fallen into a crevice in a rock, bursts it by the dynamics of its diffused power. Is this not also the case with a vital idea? Drop it into the soil of experience with no frantic concern as to its survival and see what happens. To ears that can hear, there is nothing so deafening as the detonation of an idea at the moment of its explosion. Or, on the contrary, if you choose, in the interest of conserving an idea, put it away out of reach of the tentacles of sunlight or the caresses of moisture and warmth. And see what does *not* happen! There is indeed an element of daring involved in sowing the seeds of thought. Nothing is more precious than an idea; to scatter them is like sowing pearls, or dragon's teeth. Once out of our hands they are gone, and he who loves truth cannot but feel a certain fear that their harvest, subject as it is to the caprice of wind, rain and sun may be too rashly hazarded by the hand that scatters.

When one reflects upon it, however, the fact is so simple as to be almost trivial. Is this not the basis of all our educative processes? Time was when ideas were the private monopoly of a few. When priests or pundits could proscribe the use of ideas, segregating them for a class, a caste or a cult, selfishness and fear were the doom of culture. Not only did sterility corrupt wisdom like a blight; fear corrupted its custodians. History has no surer testimony on the point than the intellectual history of Egypt. Instead of fructifying in the soil of common humanity, it was hidden away, and what remains of it now is being dug up out of the dust of the centuries. What might have happened to it otherwise is anyone's guess, but that it died and brought forth no fruit is a matter of record. If we turn to the Christian record to observe the operation of the principle in the beginnings of our culture, we are confronted at the outset by the profound word in the prologue to John's gospel: "The word became flesh and dwelt among us." Here was the Word which was the symbol of an idea, taken—in the picturesque language of the gospel—out of the austere isolation of the eternal world and set down in the soil of humanity. A seed fell into the ground to die! Again, what would have happened to the idea of God otherwise is anyone's guess, but that Jesus fructified this germinal idea in the fields of human experience is a matter of record.

The validation of the Cross principle in the region of thought rests only on the pragmatic results its operation achieves. The time capsule buried in the grounds of the World's Fair will yield no fruitage in life. For five thousand years its inviolability is assured, and the preservation of its contents guaranteed. What it can do after five millenniums no one can foresee or predict; and yet that compact cache of twentieth-century memorabilia is hardly more completely sterilized than certain fecund ideas that are today kept from the soil of human experience by the high priests of finance, government, and international affairs lest, perchance falling into the ground, they might flower into such a harvest of aspiration, hope, and renovation that the world we live in would be changed as by some divine interposition. The Cross principle in the experience of Jesus has provided *moral* redemption, for all time, wherever it has been accepted in the world. The Cross principle in the experience of thought has provided *intellectual* redemption for those whose fear of the insurgency of ideas has driven them into an infallible institution or behind a frightened conscience. It is certainly not too much to affirm that only as orthodoxy, which has often had so much to say about the Cross, releases the dynamic energy of the Cross into the area of its thought life, its ideas will remain alone, and safe, and moribund. How far, after all, are any of us willing to take the ideas that to us provide the sustenance of our spiritual life, and scatter them, relinquish them if necessary, for the life of the world. God, Christ, destiny, doom, salvation, immortality, redemption—name the ideas by which we live. Are they ours because they were preserved in capsules and transmitted to us as heirlooms? Rather are they not ours because they have fallen into the ground of the life of every generation, and brought forth harvests that have nourished and sustained the ever-famished spirit of humanity? And is there any other way to assure endless harvests as time goes on?

Nicodemus was orthodox. That detracts nothing from the undisputed nobility of his character. But all of the winsomeness of his friend from Nazareth could not constrain his loyalty because there were precious ideas that he must jealously guard. But the faith of Nicodemus, lofty and beautiful as it was, has suffered for centuries from the efforts to preserve its integrity; and the faith of Jesus, cast into the ground to die, has flowered all over the world.

Joseph of Arimathea was a good man, and rich; and like many such to this good hour, lavishly supported with money the safe orthodoxy of his noble faith. What would have happened had his money been offered in support of an idea that was to die, and then fill the earth? That is something else to wonder about. What is less a matter of speculation is what might happen in our modern world if rich men could see the Cross principle in reference to both material and intellectual wealth. Certainly the causes for which liberals often plead in vain, causes by the support of which our Christian faith will bring forth much fruit, would not languish. But unless the Cross redeems both our money and our minds, there is slight hope for material and intellectual harvest.

Perhaps the final word should deal with our ultimate hope. Nicodemus and Joseph did finally bring their loyalty into the open—they cast into the ground their pride, and it flowered at once into devotion. And what is this but another parable of the word that is eternal as the principle it pictures: "Except a grain of wheat fall into the ground and diffuse, it abides alone; but if it diffuse, it brings forth much fruit"?

CHAPTER SEVEN

Part One

THE CENTURION

In the month of January of the year when the title "Augustus" was bestowed by the Roman Senate on Gaius Octavianus, a son was born to a pious peasant family in a small village northeast of Beneventum in Central Italia. He was given the name of Octavius Domitius, and like many another male child born that year was destined by his name to help keep the memory of the great Octavian Augustus alive. The month of January had been decreed by the Senate as a period of celebration, and during those bitter winter days there was not a hut from Britain to Parthia that did not hear recited beside a kindling hearth-fire the glories of the man who, starting as a youth of twenty in Caesar's African legions had risen to become imperator, to win great renown for the imperial eagles, and wealth and security for his people, and who, after finally building a temple to himself in Rome, was to die acclaimed as a god.

As a lad Domitius grew strong in body, helping his father in the fields, and his mother was careful to see that nurture in the religion of her ancestors was a part of his daily routine. He early learned to salute Janus, the god of the door, as he came in the house; he would not eat until the deities of the store cupboard were fed, nor could he compose himself for rest without a genuflection to Vesta, goddess of the hearth. He could never forget his first attendance on the ceremonial of anticipation and prayer with which the spring was greeted. Until his mother told him its meaning, he was terrified at the slaughter of the sacrificial cow heavy with young; but even so, he remembered unpleasantly to his dying day the helpless struggle of the

159

stricken animal, and the solemn offering of the unborn calf. He enjoyed more the festivals at harvesttime, the mysterious vintage rites, and the twin celebrations to the divinity pair Consus and Ops, who gave increase to the lands and food for the barren months of winter.

Every once in so often, Roman legionaries passed through the village, or stopped off for the night in a neighbor hut. To his youthful eyes these men were more than mortals, and he wondered whether Janus could provide greater protection at a door, or Jupiter himself be more resplendent than a lictor in his uniform of leather and brass. Like most of the boys of the countryside it was his proud hope some day to join the legion, to march off to do battle with the barbarians and to return, perhaps at the head of a column, as a hero.

His mother's shrewd and solicitous eye was not blind to the stirring of these martial hopes in his young heart, nor was she wholly averse to them. To rise in the ranks of the army was an honorable ambition, and except for the hazards of war and the brutalizing influences of discipline and barrack life that left many a man hard, cruel, and insensitive to the virtues of gentler pursuits, she was not unfriendly to his dream. When therefore, as had for some months seemed inevitable, he came running home late one afternoon to announce the arrival of a recruiting officer in the village, and to ask, breathlessly, for permission to become a soldier, he was astonished that his mother smiled indulgently, and that his father clapped him smartly on the shoulder as a gesture of assent.

When, however, the time came for him to leave home, his mother, with that easy surrender to her own tears that is the invincible strength of motherhood, wept shamelessly upon him. In the little bundle of clothes she rolled up for his journey to the garrison, she hid two wooden household gods for his protection, and her only word of admonition was that he remember the gods of his fathers and be worthy of blessings they granted generously to the faithful. And he, in turn, found his voice less sure than he had thought it would be when he spoke his words of farewell, but his young heart was unshaken in the resolve to be honest, courageous, and dutiful according to the code of his newly espoused craft, and pious according to the religion of his forebears.

His mother wiped her eyes with the back of her hand as he started down the road, and perhaps his father's laugh was forced and unconvincing, but before he was lost to view, the gods granted her a promise in a moment of vision. She saw him suddenly enveloped in a glow of golden light, armed cap-a-pie as the captain of a company, leading a column in brisk, rhythmic tread. And then the light faded. She wiped her eyes again and returned his salute far down the roadway, and hurried indoors.

From the recruiting station at the garrison he was sent to Rome with a group of young men his own age, and the dis-illusionment that sooner or later seizes all youth, and that in his case was a compound of nostalgia and the rigors of army discipline, was not long deferred. He set his gods up by his hard bed in the barracks, but the derision of older men shamed him into hiding them by day, and supplicating them furtively in the darkness. He found also that the simple belief of his family in the spirits of the woods and the house had been lost in a confusion of deities of other peoples. Roman gods had Greek names and were enshrined in temples. Diana was Artemis now, Juventas was Hebe, Mars was Ares. Cybele was the Great Mother of the Gods, and in her train, instead of Jupiter, Bacchus, Isis, and Mithras followed, come hither to Rome from Egypt and Persia. But worse, to him, was the open and shameless talk that boasted the victory of philosophy over religion. The wisdom of Epicurus and the creed of the Stoics was, by men who called themselves Skeptics, the end of all trust in gods. Domitius tried to talk to his friends but those who were willing were as confused as he, and those who had no interest, laughed at him. Many was the time at the close of a day of exhausting routine in the garrison he would fall prone on his bed, and then, mindful of his promise, struggle to his knees to supplicate his gods before sleep overcame him. And as darkness laid its mantle over him he would long for the woods beyond Beneventum, and for a word of guidance and encouragement from his mother.

He was forty-one when Augustus died. For forty years Rome had been at comparative peace, and under the patronage of the great emperor, philosophy, art, and literature had prospered alongside the material wealth and security that his rule had won. Not only so; Augustus had shrewdly noted that the coalescence of Greek and Roman religions had left the common people confused, and that the rites and festivals which afford simple hearts the easiest mode of religious expression had so multiplied and overlapped that temples were sparsely visited, and festivals had become orgies of debauchery and impiety. At his suggestion, therefore, as an aid to religious revival, the Senate conferred the status of deity on his great father, Julius Caesar, and all those in the empire who were mindful of religious needs were thenceforth to worship Divus Julius as their god. It was natural, therefore, that after his devoted wife Livia reverently collected his own ashes and placed them in the mausoleum by the Tiber which he had built for his family and himself, the last act of the Senate should have been the formal decree that added Augustus to the roster of the gods recognized by the Roman state.

Domitius had done well in the legions. He had been promoted to the rank of centurion while fighting with the army of Germanicus in Dalmatia, and his reputation for courage, devotion to duty, and unflinching discipline was not confined to his own legion. Time and again he had re-enlisted when his service term was expired, and when he was fifty he was transferred, somewhat against his wish, to a Syrian legion with headquarters in Caesarea.

All during his career he had kept his promise to his mother, and yet at no time had he achieved the peace of mind that he had sought. As a dutiful citizen he had worshiped Julius, and with similar unimaginative devotion he had added Augustus to his pantheon. But a stubborn moral sensitiveness plagued his perfunctory piety when he remembered that, while Augustus had been a patron of art and religion in his latter years, he had also been noted, as a younger man, for cruelty as cynical as it was bold, and for deceptions and intrigues which a consuming and conscienceless ambition could but weakly justify. Such surely was no prelude to deity, Domitius often said to himself, nor could the formal decree of a senate expiate the sins of an emperor or raise to godhead one whose humanity had been, at times, arrogantly godless. And thus the conflict waged in the soldier's mind, a conflict between the simple faith of the countryside and the elaborate and mixed religious aspirations of the hybrid culture of Rome. Withal he failed not to address himself daily to some sort of divinity; in the morning to Vesta, in the evening to Venus, and at festivals to the deity-designate of the day. But never was his restlessness staid or the hunger of his spirit satisfied.

He was astonished to discover among the Jews a strange indifference to the confusion of deities that he had observed wherever else he had been throughout the empire. With a defiance of Roman decrees that was often dangerous, they worshiped their Jehovah in synagogue and temple, and acclaimed a rectitude of life that, while sometimes pretentious and empty, was nevertheless, among the common folk, fearless and uncompromising. He happened to be in the deep Jordan Valley one spring when a half-mad hermit from the wilderness was preaching. It was a stern and threatening doctrine, but it so interested Domitius that he turned aside from his tour of military inspection to hear his thundering words. The man knew nothing of Vesta or Augustus, but he knew a great deal about greed, hypocrisy, lasciviousness, and the fruitlessness of formal religious practices. The people were deeply moved; even soldiers from near-by garrisons were seen in the multitudes that thronged him, and officers commended the desert priest to the inspector for the renovation his words had accomplished in their restless and lusty men.

On another occasion Domitius and his bodyguard came upon a peasant preacher on the slope of a hill in Galilee. It was late evening, but the crowds still pressed upon him to hear his words. He was conferring blessing upon the poor, the sorrowful and the persecuted, and promising the beatitude of their heavenly Father to the meek and the pure and the strivers after peace. This was unlike Jupiter or Julius, and yet the people heard him gladly, for to his words of simple wisdom and encouragement, he added deeds of mercy to the sick and dispirited.

One day when he was in Jerusalem on official business he thought to visit the temple to observe the worship of these godly people. He entered the outer court during the middle of the morning. There were very few people about, for it was past the hour of worship, but he noticed that those whom he encountered looked at him haughtily. He was not unused to that, but he was surprised that no images crowded the walls as in the temples in Rome. The Court of the Gentiles had little beauty save a sort of rectilinear austerity of marble and gold, and he was on the point of entering the Court of the Women despite a warning against the admission of the un-circumcised, when he was accosted by three priests who, with a fury as reckless as it was violent, stood threateningly between him and the portal. They all shouted at him in their ancient tongue, and—though he did not know it—demanded a male-diction from Jehovah upon the Gentile dog that dared defile their holy temple. Domitius was, for a moment, inclined to make a personal issue of his right to go anywhere that the authority of Rome prevailed, but he thought better of it and allowed the priests to crowd him back into the Court of the Gentiles. He turned and departed, but in his mind there took shape a definite dislike of priests, and a disappointment with what he had seen and experienced in their sanctuary. The priests, he thought, were defending something they held sacred; the simpler folk of the countryside were living something that they found satisfying, and this was more than he had won for himself.

The feast of *Ludi Megalensis* on the fourth of April turned out to be the most important day in Domitius' life. Not that the day meant anything as a festival. It was noted on the calendar, but very little attention was given it otherwise. Furthermore, as he had grown older—he had his sixtieth birthday on January 27th, the day on which sixty years before Octavian Gaius Caesar was first called Augustus—he had wearied of the folderol of holidays. They were so completely emptied of their original meaning and prostituted to such bizarre and extravagant uses that he spent them quietly when relieved of duty, or under the strictest sort of prophylactic discipline when he had men under orders.

Megalesia that year coincided with the greatest Jewish festival—the Passover. Domitius remembered the date by the Roman calendar, but he was never to forget the day because of what happened to a certain Jew, a peasant preacher from Nazareth. To Domitius the observance of the Passover was unaccountably mixed up with the execution of this man who, by common consent and the pronouncement of the Procurator, had done nothing worthy of death. Two brigands were scheduled for crucifixion that morning and because of some sort of tie-up between the high priest and Pilate the preacher was turned over to the praetorian guard for scourging and death.

Executions were always distasteful, but as a part of the business of government had to be got on with. Perhaps they appeased justice, or fate, or Jupiter, or Jehovah, or simply provided a spectacle to satisfy a lust for blood that some said needed periodic satisfaction. In any case, the order for the death of this man went through the hands of the centurion, and, in the performance of his duty, he accompanied the process from the moment he was delivered into his hands, until he turned him over to those who claimed his lifeless body just before sunset. And from that first minute to the last, Domitius was to witness something that was utterly new and strange in all his professional experience of blood, pain and death.

There was a code that, by unanimous and subtle consent, was agreed to among the victims of judicial vengeance. They would exchange life for death, but they would drive a hard bargain, and in saying farewell to life, they would show the sort of angry defiance with which they had accepted it. No curse was too terrible and no obscenity too black for the lips of the doomed, and they vied with one another in grim contest to see which could die the most obdurate and impenitent death. But not this peasant preacher. Domitius had seen scores of scourgings. Some victims had whimpered and pled for mercy, some had burst their bonds and flung themselves upon the scourger, some had contorted like a nest of smitten vipers. This man did not cringe or boast, he did not wince or yield, he did not curse or cry. And when the master of the scourge stupidly missed his count and struck him thrice too often, the man asked that the pain of the illicit blows be allowed to expiate the error. He thanked the doctor who tended his lacerated back, and spoke only words of gentleness to the ruffians that hustled him out of the yard. Never had a man accepted punishment—and punishment admittedly unjust by official confession—as did that man. Domitius could not understand it.

The centurion was scrupulous to a fault in the performance of his duty, and he was irritated by what he thought was an unnecessary delay outside the gate as they were on their way to Skull Hill. The Galilean stumbled and fell, but his fall was broken by a man who caught the cross as it slipped from his shoulder. That a spectator should help a felon was strange enough, but it was stranger that a felon would allow it. It was a part of the code to scorn every show of pity, and to accept help was a confession of weakness; but this man asked, with a show of deep solicitude, if his benefactor felt the cross too heavy for him. As was the custom, women cried out in accusation or in pity as their sympathies dictated but instead of the lewd retort that was customarily heard, this man spoke with tender pity to those who were bereft of kin or burdened with loneliness. A hush like a sudden lull in a storm had followed his words, and faces showed a respite from anguish, and the centurion himself felt the strange pervasive lessening of tension. It was a full minute before he shook off the spell and called the cavalcade to order and to march. For the first time he found it hard to watch the brutal job of driving the nails through a man's hands. He offered no resistance to the executioners, in striking contrast to the writhing struggles of the thieves on either side of him. An hour later when the young legionary who, at his scourging in the morning had kept the score for the scourge-master, took a flask of drugged wine from a bystander and offered him a drink to dull his pain and ease the torture of dying, he declined it. This, Domitius realized later, was neither stubbornness nor bravado. The man who had made no truce with life was asking no truce with death; he who had seen clearly into the heart of humanity was loath to look into the face of God with his brain fogged by an anodyne. Into the mind of Domitius flashed pictures of the drunken orgies of those who boasted in Rome their lordship over life and laid claims to divinity, but who took flight from their own bitterness and disillusion in a draft of nepenthe or by the sting of an asp.

The taunts of the mob evoked no reply from him. He silenced the thieves who hung beside him with a quiet word. To his mother, trembling near by on the arm of a friend he spoke reassuringly, and then he prayed—not to an image in a gaudy shrine, and not with a bleeding victim freshly slain, nor with an offering for a venal priest. For those who had judged him falsely, condemned him unjustly, and slain him cruelly, he asked forgiveness, and then with a sigh that marked an epoch in the history of the world, he acknowledged the realization of his eternal destiny, and committed his soul to his father. Here was spiritual fortitude and confidence as inexplicable as his physical courage, but that was the end of him. Or was it?

A tremor rippled beneath the surface of the earth, shuddered up and over the hill and was gone. The sky above the summit, seemed to spiral upward in a black vortex and then dip in a golden whorl to the earth as if to salute the dying with a portent of heaven. The crowd on the hilltop suddenly stopped their taunting cries, lifted their faces, white with terror, to the sky, and departed silently for the city, beating their breasts. The soldiers gave up their dicing at the foot of the cross.

Domitius dropped to his knees and bowed his head in reverent wonder. Through his mind trooped a succession of figures, resplendent with the glories of the earth: Jupiter, Janus and Vesta, Cybele, Bacchus and Mithra, and last of all Julius and Augustus. He opened his eyes. The crowd was gone. A shaft of golden light broke like a flying javelin from the phalanx of dark cloud that crowded the west, and for a transforming interval illumined the center cross with a soft ethereal glow. Domitius got slowly to his feet and lifted his eyes toward the face, now passionless in death. He remembered a promise made before the door of a rude hut, many years ago, and with a sensation of fulfillment he was never able to explain said: "Truly *this* was the Son of God."

Part Two

THE CROSS AND THE WAR MIND

It is of very little importance which of the words recorded as having been spoken by the centurion regarding Jesus at the moment of his death is to be thought authentic. Matthew and Mark agree that he said, "This surely was the son of God," and marginal variations allow "a son of God" and "a son of the gods." Luke places a somewhat different emphasis: "Certainly this was a righteous man." This strange reversal of the court's verdict was too late to save the culprit but even so it was a very injudicious, not to say dangerous, remark. It followed an ascription of praise to God which may be regarded as confession of a latent faith, or of a sudden conversion, or as nothing more than a soldier's spontaneous and mildly blasphemous ejaculation. John's gospel omits the episode entirely.

But it is important that this pagan said something so extraordinary as to merit a place in the record. Perhaps he changed his mind about Jesus and his guilt. It happens in nearly every criminal case that some few remain unconvinced that the court has judged correctly. If this is the meaning of his comment it is interesting but hardly significant. Perhaps he changed his mind about God. Occasionally human behavior —notably in death—does have the effect of altering the theological presuppositions of an observer, and as such his words would be both interesting and significant. But if his remark indicates a change of view concerning the final meaning of life, we are faced with something weighty with implications.

Not that the military mind, of which this man may reasonably be regarded as representative, is any harder to change than any other type. On basal issues, any mind is hard to change; if it changes easily it is something other than mind! But if within the space of hardly more than half a day, under conditions that normally would have broken the strongest body and the stoutest heart, Jesus behaved in such a manner as could focus a pagan mind on deity, and at the same time suggest so intimate a connection between a dying man and an undying God as the phrase Son of God (or a son of the gods) implies, the death of Jesus must have been as decisive for the soldier as his life had been for Simon Peter (cf. Matthew 16:16). Whatever his judgment was, we cannot properly regard it as theological. If it is to be described by a single word, "moral" is likely to be as near to the officer's mind as we can get.

The moral assumptions of the military mind are both articulate and organized. It regards history as the record of conquests, conquest as a matter of subjugating an enemy, and an enemy as one who must be destroyed because he cannot be conciliated. This puts it rather baldly and in outline it appears little short of brutal. But in spite of the insistence by the makers of war that they loathe their job and do it only because it is necessary, they consent to it only because it makes sense to their view of the world. Therefore personality is subject to judgment by court-martial and man's primary virtue is muscular heroism. To wince at the pain one feels or to scruple at the pain one inflicts is a man's shame, though it may be a woman's glory.

It is proper to assume that such was the background of the centurion's experience. His ideas of deity may have been metaphysically hazy, but morally they were fairly clear. Jupiter riding the sky in his chariot drawn by four white horses, waving his scepter over rain, hail and thunder, was no sissy. To capture the wild bull of Minos, and slay the Nemean lion with bare hands, Hercules needed more than the wisdom of the sibyls. Achilles was slain because his doting mother held his heel when she dipped him in the prophylactic waters of the Styx, otherwise he might have been immortal. Such gods as the centurion had heard about were heroes. Sometimes they mingled too intimately with mortals, and they always lost something by it; something about the human touch softened them. So if there were a supreme deity, as the Jews taught, he was surely the compendium of all heroisms, unsullied by mortal weakness. Indeed was not the Jehovah of the Jews the God of Battles? He had been, so they said, in the days of their great power.

And yet by such standards this dying Nazarene seemed very little like a god. Far from it. Gods were immortal and conferred immortality on their offspring, and this man was dead. Gods were bold and terrible in their anger, but this man had suffered unspeakable tortures without so much as a threat, and instead of anger, his pain had inspired forgiveness for his enemies. Had gods been created in men's minds after the pattern of this man's uncomplaining suffering and his stubborn will to forgive instead of to destroy his executioners, what a strange pantheon would have peopled the empyrean! So inexplicable this soldier's verdict has appeared that he has been thought to have been a secret disciple of the Galilean, or a member of a "devout" cult, many of which flourished throughout the empire. He can be explained on almost any grounds except those of his military faith. In the light of all for which he stood, he must be judged as an apostate to his craft. To his remark: this surely was the Son of God, the obvious reply was: and you surely are no soldier.

This is not to say that soldiers have not and do not believe in God, or in his Son. That libel has been cast at the military profession, and nothing is more unjust or unkind. But military men, brought up under the broad influences of the Christian tradition, and loyal to its conventional and creedal forms are in a position very different from the centurion. He contradicted his conventional faith to give loyal assent to its opposite. A modern parallel would be for a Christian soldier to extol the virtues of Gautama as credentials for his promotion in rank from corporal to colonel.

Without appearing to draw from his confession what we ourselves might put into his words, we may be allowed to ask what, in the light of the present, his statement may imply. In the first place, the sense of deity is implicit. In so far as a belief in the existence of God lies at the heart of what most of us understand by the word religion, the centurion confessed a religious faith. Indeed, as one of the gospels puts it, "he glorified God." What God has come to mean to the life and thought of the last thirty centuries is beyond our present concern. We can be content with a bare minimum. God has always represented something above the level on which the believer moves. This is so universal a fact that for philosophical or primitive theisms it is basal. It is negatively implicit even in atheism, for the atheist does not believe in God because he does not believe in a level of being higher than his own. Once he hypothecates such a level, it must be made known by the objects it encloses, and if these hypothetical objects partake of the superior qualities of the medium in which they move, they must be super-creatures. It is no surprise that atheism is at war with supernaturalism, as the idea is sometimes uncritically used.

But to the centurion the fact of God was validated by the dying of Jesus less in a metaphysical than in a moral sense. If God was something higher than himself, he was something morally higher than himself. Consequently he would have discovered, had he stopped to reflect upon it, that God's reactions to human behavior might be of a quality higher than the human. Where the normal human reaction to hate would be hate, the normal divine reaction might be love. Setting aside for the moment the question whether love *is* a higher reaction than hate—since in our modern world there is strong feeling and vigorous dispute on the point—we are right in assuming that to the centurion it must have appeared to be, and to those of us who accept the Christian tradition, it *must* be. The moment hate outranks love in the scale of Christian virtues, virtue to the Christian will no longer have meaning. That this has taken place in certain parts of the world is one of the appalling facts that the growth of militarism forces upon us.

Pressing our inference a step further we may assume that if Jesus was regarded as the son of God, he partook of his moral nature (we still think the centurion was not deeply concerned with metaphysics), and therefore his behavior, from the moment he was turned over to the praetorian guard, till he was seen to die, conformed to the moral prescriptions of divinity. Like father like son was a deduction simple to make, and it was more obvious then than the one we make now. We say like son, like father: God must be like Jesus. To the centurion the proposition was reversed.

If God represented a moral level higher than man's, he also represented a moral purpose higher than man's, for except as an act is related to a purpose it has no moral significance. Every act of God was to be judged as right or wrong in terms —so to speak—of its relation to his ultimate will. If an act advanced that purpose it was right; if it retarded it, it was wrong. God's will is therefore to be achieved by those who share his purpose, and their conduct will be judged solely by that standard. No arbitrary code improvised by man to meet an emergency need can claim moral validity unless it conforms to the larger understanding of God's ultimate purpose. To those who believe that purpose to be beneficent and redemptive, all judgments will be rendered in such a light. To those who believe that purpose to be malign and destructive, all attitudes and actions that strengthen the forces of malignity and desolation will have the sanctions of virtue upon them. In other words, God's will for the universe is higher than man's will for himself, and therefore better. But man can participate in that higher purpose if he will conform his will to God's and judge his behavior as good or bad in terms of such conformity. Jesus demonstrated in the most critical hours of his life how God's will proposes to meet the most critical issues of life. When one faces desertion by friends, suspicion and distrust by socially and religiously respectable folk, and hate by callous or perverse or stupid people, what must one do? The answer was given the centurion on the level of human life by a human personality; and the performance was so baffling that it could only be described as the behavior of the Son of God. We must not allow ourselves to forget that Jesus was known to the centurion in the experience of tragedy. It would have been one thing to pass judgment upon him in the idyllic surroundings of lilies and birds and little children; it was profoundly another thing to judge him in the shadow and in the torture of the cross. Not until we can pass through tragedy with a sense of the will of God, and with its searching moral judgment on our acts, can we claim for ourselves the exalted title of sons of God. Does this not cast light on one of Jesus' most famous words: "Blessed are the peacemakers, for they shall be called the children of God"? Peace that is *made* according to God's will out of the cruelty and anger of men—it is on those who do that that beatitude rests.

To sum up: the eternal God, in the experience of a human personality, was reacting according to his moral nature in a desperate moral crisis within the framework of time. The centurion was putting it with elemental simplicity when he said: Surely this (this sort of response to this particular situation) is what one can understand as the authentic behavior of the Son of God. To state it for ourselves: God is in history working out his moral purpose by means of human personalities. His will is orderly, beneficent and pacific. In the experience of Jesus we have a demonstration of the way by which God, opposed by disorder, malevolence, and death proposed to bring peace, and love, and life to fulfillment in human affairs.

But this sort of thing did not come to pass by wishing it were so. Allied with the moral purposes of God is the power to bring it to pass. Once again, without loading the simple testimony of the centurion with the freight of our reflections, it can be said, without violence to the total situation, that he must have been impressed by the power this dying man manifested. Surely nothing is less plausible than to argue that it was weakness that impressed him with the divine sonship of Jesus. And it was power that was displayed within the medium of physical weakness. No portent or prodigy of physical strength called forth the accolade. It was not until physical power was spent and death had supervened that the man appeared as the Son of God. Can it be that the flash of insight that penetrated the darkness of Calvary's summit and illumined the mind of the officer with a sense of the moral *purpose* of God, also communicated to him the real nature of the *power* of God? If so, we discover still deeper meaning in his words.

There is no question as to what a Roman legionary regarded as the ultimate of power. Politically it was the empire, built upon the military genius of Julius Caesar and the invincible phalanxes that had extended and subjugated its borders. Morally it was the sword that could compel obedience and constrain to order. But Jesus represented no such power. He had neither political party nor sword. On the contrary he abjured both. "My kingdom is not of this world"; "put up your sword." What was his strength?

There has been no little confusion concerning the morality of the use of power. Those who refuse to employ aggressive physical power as a political resource are said to be advocates of impotence and inaction. This is due to the failure to see that there are at least two types of power available to human use. For the sake of simplicity they may be called physical and spiritual. To say that the use of power is immoral is to say that God is immoral, for he is power. Paul would never have espoused a powerless gospel; he was not ashamed of the gospel because it was the power of God unto salvation to everyone that believeth. And in that word "believeth" we have an essential moral distinction of greatest importance. The gospel is not the power of God unto salvation to everyone that is defeated by it; but to those who consent to it. Its power is that which evokes consent, not subjugates. This is to say that it is spiritual power.

The question therefore of the morality of force depends upon the nature of the force to be employed. God uses force to achieve his will; but if his will is beneficent and orderly, only such force as issues in gentleness and peace is morally valid. His force may be a great idea, or the manifestation of a great love, and if the idea and love are his, they are as omnipotent as he is and ultimately will prove invincible. The great error of humankind has been that it has thought that because physical force, seen within a narrow perspective, sometimes appears to be measurably effective in achieving tranquillity and freedom of life, it is therefore morally or spiritually competent to achieve ultimately the will of God. Unless the final consummation of the divine purpose is to be the victory of spiritual force, there can be no ground for the claim that that purpose is a moral one.

To say that war has accomplished spiritual ends and achieved moral values is to mistake eddies in the stream of history for the main current. Without Cromwell there would have been no democracy, without Luther no Reformation, without the War between the States no union. This we are endlessly told and the lesson is clear: we must fight for democracy, religious freedom and national solidarity with physical weapons, and they will bring us victory in the future as they have in the past. It is easily overlooked, however, that it was the spirit and urgency of democracy that brought

Cromwell into power, not Cromwell who created the spirit of self-government. Granted that spirit, which we may call one aspect of the will of God in history, would it not have worked itself out in time by methods of which Cromwell was impatient? Cromwell was an eddy in a stream, a temporary wresting of God's purpose in order that by methods God cannot use, it might be sooner brought to pass. Similarly there is strong historic basis for the belief that had the impetuous Luther been willing to follow the more gradual and pacific moral renovations that Erasmus and More were already winning within the body of the church, the Reformation would have been achieved without the schism that still scandalizes Christendom and the Thirty Years' War that is a blot upon the pages of history. And what student of American history doubts that the differences between the states were already in the first stage of settlement because responsible men had seen the economic fallacy of slavery? It was the haste of irresponsible political leadership that precipitated that needless and tragic episode in our national life. The interpretation of history as the conquest of evils by physical violence is the military fallacy that so many have accepted. It mistakes the detour for the highway; the impatience and frenzy of men for the calm and undefeatable purposes of the Eternal.

But is there no place in time for physical force? The realities of history demand something more immediately effective than the long-term operations of eternity. Yes, one inclines to say, but only up to the point of restraint on evil. The moment physical force violates or paralyzes spiritual force in oneself or in another, it becomes immoral. It becomes demonic, no matter how exalted its protestations of virtue. Few things are more obviously taught by history than that this actually comes to pass. One may restrain another against peril or folly, but one cannot destroy another to prevent him from acting the fool. Such is police power. But police power is *not* police power when it destroys the disturber of public peace. In that

act it becomes penal; and that confuses the whole issue. The
affixing of a penalty for wrongdoing is essentially a spiritual
undertaking—or should be; the restraint of a wrongdoer up to,
but short of the point of inflicting penalty, is the proper
prerogative of physical force.

It is the fact that physical violence immobilizes all our
spiritual forces that so appalls us. It is more appalling even
than the physical destruction of war, for upon it the maintenance and extension of spiritual power and the permanence
of the race ultimately rests. The progress of the race has never
depended on violence, for violence always destroys the principle of consent by which progress alone is possible. The
more violence, the less consent; the less consent, the more
violence. Just now we are in a phase of human history in
which the trust in violence as the only adequate force is all
but universal; and yet the more we trust it, the more we
imperil the civilization that was built without it, and that can
endure only if the madness is purged from our breasts. That
we trust that larger good will emerge from this temporary
wickedness is to ignore the witness of history and to deceive
ourselves. It is war that creates and sustains the things that
make war inevitable. War to end war is like starvation to cure
hunger. The dreadful delusion that physical violence can
alone destroy physical violence possesses our minds in spite
of psychology that says: to be a successful destroyer one must
hate well; and to hate well one must abandon the restraints
of reason; and of religion that says: except a grain of wheat
fall into the ground and diffuse, it will not fructify. The
tendency of modern civilization is in the direction of making
spiritual harvest impossible; and the famine that threatens
the hearts of men is more terrible than that which threatens
their stomachs.

Machiavelli said: "Always act toward your enemy as though
one day he may be your friend." That is good sense on the
purely empirical level, though we seem to have dispensed

with it. We are about come to the place where we are convinced our enemy cannot ever be our friend, therefore we must exterminate him. Jesus said, in so many words: "Always act toward your enemy as though he *were* your friend." That is good common sense, but it lies on a level higher than the Machiavellian. It assumes that one is not to wait until something happens to convert him from an enemy to a friend, we must make it our business to win him. "If thine enemy hunger feed him!" Of course we have abandoned this impractical sort of dreaming. But when Jesus, encircled by a cordon of hate and scorn and fury and death, prayed that it might be forgiven, he treated his enemies as though they were friends, and lo, at the moment of his dying, the man who had supervised his agony and made certain his death, bowed his head and confessed him to be the Son of God. No cynicism can discount that victory of spiritual power over physical violence; and no code improvised to take us through a crisis of terror and pain, can replace the law to which it was obedient. One may be allowed to wonder whether during the outpouring of the Spirit at Pentecost there were not many who, leaving Skull Hill that day beating their breasts in contrition, were to turn in devotion to him, who, when all the fury of hell broke over and about him, opened his lips only to ask for forgiveness for those who believed their hatred was righteous, and their scorn was a form of godliness. Nor can one leave the scene without registering the feeling that the force we must have today to save the world from suicide is the power of those who are willing to live by a code that affirms and demonstrates the moral intentions of God and the invincibility of the spirit. They, by the express word of Jesus, will also merit the praise the centurion uttered in the presence of its greatest manifestation twenty centuries ago. They too will be called the sons of God.

There is perhaps one other thing that should be said. We

dare not affirm that the centurion's acclaim was his epitome of a well-wrought religious faith. As suggested above, it is possible that it was no more than an ejaculation. Certainly it would have been nothing short of miraculous had he been able, amid the welter of those few hours, to compose a living and energizing faith. We may, if we wish, speculate on what happened to him in the years that followed. Did his apparent repudiation of the military mind issue in his demit from the legion? Here is material for a story that must be passed over now. If we may raise a point relevant to our own state of mind today, what might the relation of this confession of his be to the sum of his philosophy of life? Is the refusal to participate in the use of the type of force that is costly, disruptive and finally suicidal, an article of faith, or is it the body of faith?

Obviously the burden of this discussion has been that the cross of Jesus was a demonstration of his faith in the ultimate victory of spiritual power over sin even in its most horrid form. It was not the only such demonstration. "Nothing in his life became him like the leaving it" was spoken of the Thane of Cawdor, not of Christ. Many things in life became him like the leaving of it, for one principal animated all he did. If then his life was all of one pattern, can we who affirm the Cross principle to be the dynamic of the cosmos be content to make the refusal to use physical violence a contingent or provisional faith? It is at this point that there is much searching of heart, and rightly so. There are many who during the past twenty years stoutly advocated the pacifist position with reference to war. But in recent months that faith has faltered, and some have turned back. Not without real anguish of spirit; on the contrary, they have turned their faces away from the vision of loveliness and steeled themselves to gaze again upon the hideous face of violence. Now, we are told one should renounce such idealism in the presence of the new menace to civilization. Just because we were duped twenty-five years ago is no reason for us to believe that we are again the victims of chicanery and intrigue. Each episode in history demands a re-examination of our philosophies and readjustments, if necessary, to meet new circumstances.

There is something to be said for this, but it is most urgently advocated by those who have held the pacifist faith simply *qua* pacifism. To those who do not divide between their pacifist views and the body of their faith, to whom, that is, the Cross principle is absolute and applies to *all* of life or to *none* of it, the situation is different. To them Christian pacifism is no bright satellite revolving about the parent sun of one's faith, in danger of being exploded out of its orbit by a cataclysm. It is rather of the very essence of the sun itself. To some it is a black spot on the corona; but it can be no more blasted out of the sun than the sun itself can be blasted out of the sky. So if it is lost, the sun too has gone, and the darkness that follows is cold and terrible. If it is abandoned for lesser but more facile illumination, it will be found to have carried with it all the bright components that have hitherto warmed and fructified life.

For Jesus the Cross was the symbol of achievement, and despite the theological differences that years of reflecting upon it have evolved and discarded, it still is the sign in which his followers expect to conquer. Little wonder then that it was on the cross that the centurion saw the fact and the meaning of God. We have kept the symbol but substituted pagan ideas of courage, ideas derived from combat and man's endless struggle for power. But when we return to the Cross for our ideas of courage, we find that heroism changes before our eyes. Instead of striking the other cheek, it becomes turning the other cheek; instead of plotting against our enemies, it becomes praying for them.

This is strong medicine, so strong, perhaps that the sick world would rather die than drink it. Can we, indeed, drink the cup that he drank, and undergo the baptism that he accepted? Perhaps we need the courage to be cowards, or at least the courage to be called cowards. The Cross was a stumbling block to the Jew, said Paul, and foolishness to the Greek. It is cowardice to the American.

But to the captain of a hundred men who watched a Galilean die outside the Damascus gate it was no stumbling block. It was the steppingstone to God.

CONCLUSION

CONCLUSION

These shared his cross, but only as spectators. There is no clear record to prove that the experience of Jesus induced any of them to share the Cross as an experience. Herein lies a very important matter.

The lictors who initiated the ritual of death in the praetorium may have had moments in later years when the memory of that silent and unprotesting sufferer returned to rebuke their brutality, but there is no indication that their natures were softened or their cruelties abated. If Simon of Cyrene did what in fancy our episode concerning him suggested, it is because one thinks that the Cross should have made its power felt over his imagined wealth; but there is not even a dim tradition to intimate that it was so. The reticence of the New Testament concerning the fortunes of our Lord's family need not be taken to mean that his brothers and sisters and mother lived in perplexity and silence all their days; but one cannot quiet the impulse that asks significant questions about them. The two malefactors, to be sure, did share his death on their own crosses, but it is not strange that their crucifixion has never been allowed to rest on the moral level his has occupied for centuries. Their involuntary and defiant anguish has never been invoked as a saving grace. Did the youth from Nain go back to his village to "go off the deep end" for a great ideal? And what of Nicodemus and Joseph? Nicodemus won immortality as the host of the young rabbi one never-to-be-forgotten evening: but Joseph played too brief a part to assure him anything more than a name.

> Strange quiet man, what impulse in your breast
> Invoked your kindness to the master whom
> You had not dared to join? He wanted rest
> Within your heart, but found it in your tomb.

> Did you not dare to love him, he who sought
>   To give you life, nor asked your recompense?
> What pity that in finding him you brought
>   Your laggard love in death's cold cerements.

The centurion was overwhelmed by a demonstration of sheer spiritual fortitude and the victory it won, but, as we asked in the last chapter, did he resign his commission, and become a crusader for pacifism? Hardly. It is one thing to share a cross; it is another thing to bear one.

We return to the proposition which has unified all these studies: the Cross principle supplies the meaning of the universe. Support for this claim has been adduced only from the incidents surrounding the crucifixion of Jesus. It would not be difficult to adduce intimations of the same fact from the important fields of biology, psychology, and history. Such an effort would, however, lead us far beyond the limits we have allowed ourselves. And this Cross principle was put in the metaphorical language of Jesus as the diffusion into new life that follows the falling of a grain of wheat into the ground. This, we have said, is only one of a number of similes that are employed to convey the meaning of the cosmic idea.

That the Cross was so understood by the writers of the New Testament (except for the gospels it is referred to only by Paul and the author of Hebrews) is obvious. Paul, one can easily imagine, had to resist the temptation to rationalize—and was not always successful in doing so. He told his friends in Corinth that he had come to them with a gospel unadorned with sophistication (*ouk en sophia logou*) lest the Cross be emptied of meaning. Clearly his fear was that to yield to the tendency to theologize the experience of Jesus might result in emptying it of its profound moral significance. But even so, he did not hesitate to set it in its cosmic context. Listen to him as he writes to the Ephesians: "Having abolished in his flesh the enmity . . . that he might create in himself of the two one new man, so making peace; and might reconcile them both in one body unto God through the cross" (Ephesians 2:15-16) ; or in a similar vein to the Colossians: "peace through the blood of his cross; through him, I say, whether things upon earth or things in the heavens" (Colossians 1:20) ; or again, to the Philippians as he gives the cosmic history of Jesus, so to speak, from his *kenosis* to his *pleroma* (Philippians 2:5-11) . There is reach, both up and down, in the Cross as he saw it.

And yet one may be allowed to say that we have not heeded the warning Paul gave. Perhaps we cannot be thought wholly to blame, since he found it difficult himself. It is always easier to speculate upon a principle than to act on it. One may be a profound student of the Constitution of the United States and at the same time find it hard to grant the rights of free speech to a man who insists on talking nonsense. And so, if we have emptied the Cross of some of its moral quality and become expert in its philosophical treatment, we have only failed as it is human to fail.

It is when we get back to Jesus, however, that we find the moral challenge of the Cross set forth in uncompromising terms. That he saw the Cross principle as the cosmic order seems perfectly clear; but he did not so present it to his followers. Nor is this strange, since he spoke always in parables easy to understand. To the simplest mind the picture of a grain of wheat conveyed meaning, and its importance was no less than the importance of the harvests that sustained their meager lives.

When he spoke about a cross as symbolic of the Cross principle, he was both direct and unambiguous. Only once did he use the simile of a cross as the principle by which life is to be governed. In Matthew's account (10:38) it occurs in connection with the disaffection that was likely to arise within the circle of the family. Moffatt translates: ". . . and any one who does not take up his cross and *follow where I lead* is not worthy of me." Mark 8:34 puts it: ". . . if any one wishes to follow me let him *renounce self* and take up his cross and *so* be my follower." Luke's account (9:23) reads: ". . . if any one wishes to follow me, let him renounce self and take up his cross *day by day* and so be my follower." The italics indicate three significant emphases which must not be lost sight of: once one has accepted his own cross, he must renounce self; he must follow; and it must be a day by day experience. In other words the Cross is a directed daily discipline. Not something to be *done* at least once a day; but something that gives the quality that distinguishes one who follows him.

It is obvious then, that the cross of Jesus and the cross of each of his followers was a symbol of the Cross of the Cosmos. The sign manual fixed to the pledge of one's loyalty was not an admission of the need for Jesus to carry a cross, but *the actual cross-bearing of those who dared follow* him. "He that does not bear his own cross is not worthy of me." To accept the Cross of Christ has been, for most people, to assent to a theological dogma. To Jesus it was a moral discipline that he accepted and that was equally binding on all who consented to his leadership. The cross which he carried was not alone a part of destiny; it was a part of the discipline by which, in the profound insight of the author of Hebrews (2:10) the author of salvation was made perfect. It seems strange to say that the Cross had first to be redemptive for him before it could be redemptive through him, but such is the intimation of the familiar words. We have hesitated to say that the Cross was redemptive in his experience, but he felt its compulsion and accepted it. What, one may ask, would have happened to him had he turned his face and retreated from it? The alternatives were clearly before him and he chose. It was when the choice began to press upon his spirit that he assured himself that only as the grain fell into the ground was its final fruitage assured.

It would seem to follow then that in a very real sense, the

cross we must bear is the same sort of cross he bore. From that it would follow that we can be agents in the cosmic redemption if—and only if—we do what he did. Does this mean that there is no difference in the cross of Christ and the cross of the Christian? From the purely physical aspect an answer may be easily given. For most of us a cross will not involve the mortal agony that he suffered. But this does not exclude the possibility of physical suffering greater than his. One who sought to prove his voluntary suffering to be greater than Jesus' would thereby give evidence of a lack of moral sensitiveness to the meaning of the Cross. For the experience is not to be identified by the aggregate or acuteness of the physical pain involved, but by the moral sensitiveness that induces the willingness to go to any physical limits in order to share in the redemptive processes of God. If the Cross is pancosmic there can be no qualitative difference in the cross of Christ and the cross his follower carries. It is this profound fact that makes it possible for us not only to be redeemed by the Cross, but to be redeemers by the Cross. And this is exactly—we think—what our Lord meant when he uttered that daring and baffling word: "He that believes on me, the course of action or process I am engaged in shall also engage him" (John 14:12). The context discloses that he was not talking about "signs"; he was talking rather about his relation to the plan of redemption which he shared with his heavenly Father.

It is interesting that Paul never spoke of himself as bearing a cross. This may seem strange in the light of his ardent devotion to the living Christ. It may be explained by two facts: first, he used another simile; he spoke of himself as a voluntary slave of Christ. This was, to him an effective and dramatic way of putting the Cross principle in words. Voluntary enslavement of one's self is a redemptive act if it is done with a view to saving others. In the second place, Paul may have shunned the danger of a morbid glorification of his sufferings by using a different metaphor. "God forbid that I should glory save in the cross of Christ" (Galatians 6:14). It may have been humility that prompted such a word; it was certainly due to no lack of understanding of the cross that he had to bear daily as an agency of grace and redemption.

Such an understanding of the Cross as a personal redemptive and redeeming discipline leaves the heart numb, perhaps. Is it not morbid, psychopathic, to say that life is to reach fulfillment only by the way of the Cross? Such is the verdict of the modern age to which suffering is hateful and morally repugnant. Herein lies the dilemma in which our age is caught. We are enormously clever in the elimination of physical discomforts. Health, ease, comfort are fast getting to the point of regulation by medicines, constant temperatures, and paved roads. To court discomfort deliberately is so weird a mental illness that it has been given a name equally weird—masochism. How, indeed, can an age in which every ingenuity is dedicated to the mitigation of physical discomfort be expected to look with favor on a moral principle that proposes the redemption of the race by means of voluntary suffering accepted as the means of spiritual restitution? Does not the moral demand of the cosmos run exactly counter to the physical demands of the race?

We do not propose to resolve the dilemma.[1] It is only necessary to point out a very practical fact. The world, with its pursuit of comfort and security and wealth has gone astray morally. Is there any connection between aggrandizement and war, between our pursuit of ease and our retreat from moral rigor? What in the current scene leads us to believe that the way of the Cross is morally impotent? What indeed leads us

[1] For the author's attempt to resolve the dilemma, the reader is referred to his discussion, "The Dilemma of Civilization," in *Preaching in These Times*: The Lyman Beecher Lectures, 1940. Charles Scribner's Sons.

to believe that anything else *can* redeem us? The grain of wheat must still fall into the ground and diffuse.

This is a hard saying, and against it we instinctively and rationally rebel. But to whom else can we go? When Simon Peter asked Jesus that question, there was a ready answer he might have given: "Follow the multitude." Crowds of people had been fed on the hillside, and then Jesus began to talk to them about strange things: they must eat the flesh of the Son of Man and drink his blood if they were to have life in them. This is another simile of the Cross principle as it applied to his enactment of it and their acceptance of it; and they said it was a hard saying. Having so disposed of the matter, they began to leave the place and when all but his twelve intimates had gone, he gave them the chance to follow the retreat over the hill. "Will you also go away?" That was the easy thing to do in the face of a hard saying. Peter's reply was as profound as it is famous: "Thou hast the words of eternal life, and we have believed and know that thou art the holy one of God" (John 6:68-69).

We do not need to ask whether that lovable and tempestuous spirit put into his words all that we profess to find there. But this much can be said: in face of a hard choice, he reached for the high and the eternal. The Holy One of God represented the highest man can know; the words of eternal life represented the farthest man can see. Altitude and perspective! How different from the descent to the plain and the concern for the next meal that actuated the multitudes.

Perhaps it is too much to expect, but we must not allow cynicism to destroy our ultimate hope. Is there something in the spirit of man that eternally reaches up to the highest and looks out to the farthest? "Ceiling absolute, visibility unlimited" is the way the dispatcher in the tower describes perfect weather to the pilot ready to fly. We are grounded by bad weather for the moment, but the clouds will not always shroud the earth. If we do not choose the best it may be that we are only morally diffident, or at worst are, for the moment, morally afraid. He who, in the moment of dying, commended his spirit to his Father, had told his friends the night before, that by the choice he had made, he had overcome the world. Who can dispute that conquest, even in this dark hour? And who can miss the continuing contagion of his courage as he bade his friends in that hour to "be not afraid"?

Those who share his cross, not as spectators, but as participators—it is they alone who shall share both the redemptive purpose and the redemptive power that "will not fail nor be discouraged until he have set justice in the earth; and the isles shall wait for his law" (Isaiah 42:4).

THE END